I0818482

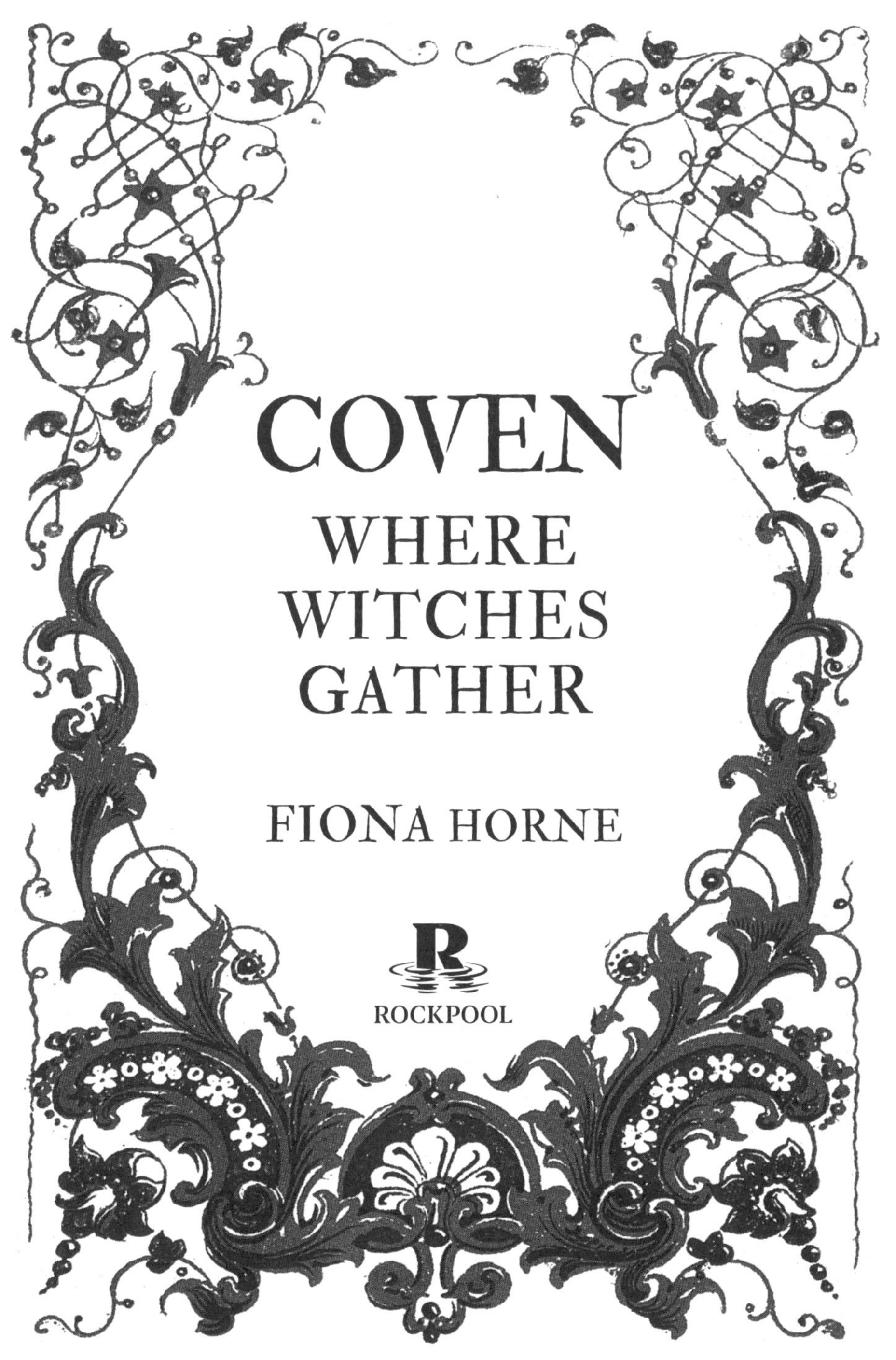

COVEN

WHERE WITCHES GATHER

FIONA HORNE

ROCKPOOL

A Rockpool book
PO Box 252
Summer Hill
NSW 2130
Australia

rockpoolpublishing.com
Follow us! rockpoolpublishing
Tag your images with #rockpoolpublishing

ISBN: 9781923208469

Published in 2026 by Rockpool Publishing

Design and typesetting by Sara Lindberg, Rockpool Publishing
Edited by Erin Della Mattia
Illustration page 204: Shutterstock

A catalogue record for this book is available from the National Library of Australia

Printed and bound in China

10 9 8 7 6 5 4 3 2 1

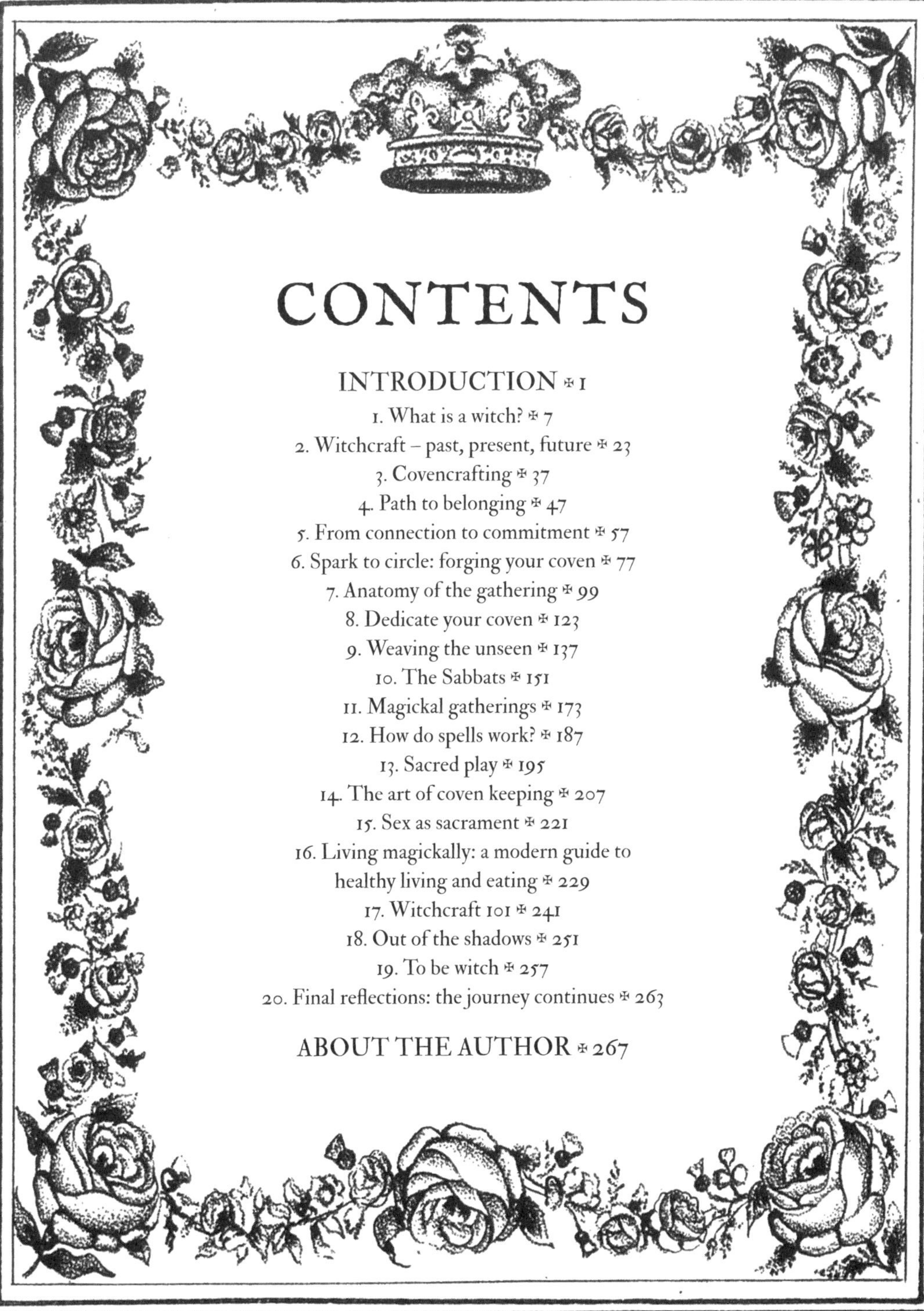

CONTENTS

INTRODUCTION

A LETTER FROM A WITCH, THEN AND NOW

Twenty years ago, I wrote a letter that opened the first edition of this book. It was a kind of spell in itself - a heartfelt offering from a girl named Fiona who had just moved to America, come out publicly as a witch, and was daring to imagine that her craft could meet the world unapologetically.

Back then, I wrote from a place of raw hope. I was fresh off a whirlwind career in rock music, having toured with the likes of Soundgarden, Smashing Pumpkins, and No Doubt. My band, Def FX, had charted; MTV had played our videos; and yet behind the stage dives and 'grrrl power', I was quietly practicing witchcraft. I wore my pentacle on album covers, dropped esoteric clues in lyrics, but never came fully out of the broom closet until the band ended and I wrote my first book. That was *Witch: A Personal Journey* in 1997. And it changed everything.

At that time, there was no social media. No Instagram, no TikTok. Witchcraft was still whispered about, still misunderstood, still veiled in fear or fantasy. It felt radical - dangerous even - to say the word witch on morning television. It felt sacred. And I took it seriously.

In the years that followed, I became a public face of the craft in ways that were both exhilarating and complicated. I was featured in *Playboy USA*. I starred in the reality show *Mad Mad House*. I was booked on Entertainment Tonight and talk shows, praised and picked apart in equal measure. I became the "hot witch," the TV witch, the pop witch. And at that time, that was necessary. Witchcraft needed a woman unafraid to stand in the glare of the mainstream and say, "We are here. We are wise. We are not evil or imaginary." I had already built a platform in music and television - it made sense that I used it. And I don't regret a moment of it.

That girl I was - green, unbeaten, fiercely optimistic - she had a role to play in the evolution of the modern craft. And she played it with every ounce of her being.

But time works its own magick. Since then, I've walked many lives. I became a world-record-holding skydiver. I became a commercial pilot and flew planes across the Caribbean delivering aid and rescuing animals. I lived in wild, beautiful places, always guided by the same unseen hand. I've spoken at Harvard on witchcraft in pop culture. I've written more books, and mentored more witches than I can count. And I now live in Egypt, leading sacred adventures for women who want to meet themselves fully in the places where the ancient gods and goddesses still speak. Through every incarnation, I've remained a witch - not because I wear the title, but because the path has always walked itself through me.

Today, witchcraft is everywhere. It's a TikTok hashtag, a lifestyle aesthetic, a booming section in bookstores and on online platforms. And that's not a criticism. We are living in an age of access, when spiritual knowledge is flowing like water, fast and wide. But with that comes dilution. Confusion. Performance. Commodity.

That's why this new edition of *Coven* matters more than ever. Because beneath the hashtags and highlight reels there is still a living, breathing mystery - a sacred, subversive truth that belongs to witches; a truth about power, connection, and the unseen forces that shape our world. This book isn't just a how-to. It's a lived testament to community, courage, and the magick we create when we gather in trust and intention.

When I first formed a coven in Los Angeles, I was just looking for soul kin. Hollywood was loud and shiny and often soul-sapping. I needed something real. I found it in Tri, my first covener - regal, humble, proud to be both Black and witchy at a time when neither was widely accepted. Then came Lupita, bringing Santería and deep ancestral magick. We weren't a traditional coven. We were intuitive. Organic. Feminine. Fierce. And it worked. That's the spirit this book embodies: not rigid lineage nor elitist secrecy, but radical trust in the divine feminine flow.

In those early years, I wrestled with guilt. Was I making witchcraft too public? Too palatable? Was I watering it down by bringing it to the masses? I've come to understand that the craft

evolves when it's ready. What I offered back then was a doorway - an invitation. Not a spectacle, but a spark.

These days, I've earned the label of elder. Not by age, but by time in service. And service is what this book ultimately is. It's a lantern held up for those seeking kindred spirits, a mirror for those finding their power, and a reminder that magick is both deeply personal and profoundly collective.

I once described this book as a guide to "getting into witchcraft, feeling magickal, and being together . . . now." That still holds. But now, I would add: being real. In a world of constant broadcast, realness is rare. This book invites you to bring your whole self - messy, magnificent, unsure, electric - to the circle. To trust that you don't have to know everything. You just have to be willing to listen, love, learn, and lead - sometimes all at once.

Witchcraft is not a performance. It's a remembrance. Of the earth. Of your body. Of the power you hold and the responsibility that comes with it.

And if you've ever wondered if you belong here - if you're "witchy enough" - let me say this: If you're asking the question, you probably already are.

Welcome to *Coven*.

This is your circle now.

Blessed Be,

Fiona

"At first, I thought being a witch was about the spells I had to learn . . . the peers I had to please. But over time, I realized it was about what I had to unlearn – the rules, the roles, the fear. Witchcraft helped me cast off everything that wasn't truly mine, so I could live a life of adventure, of freedom . . . a life of my own."

- FIONA HORNE

CHAPTER 1

WHAT IS A WITCH?

Before we talk about gathering witches together, let's consider what a witch is in the 2020s . . .

A witch is the woman standing next to you in line at the supermarket, the man sitting next to you on the train, and the girl waving hello to her friends at school. Modern witches are just that - modern. Witches have always worn many faces. Across time, place, and tradition, they shape-shift - keepers of old secrets, makers of new magick. There is no one way to look like a witch . . . only countless ways to *be* one.

Today's witchcraft community includes influential figures such as Pam Grossman, known for her books and the popular podcast, *The Witch Wave*, and Lucy Cavendish, a prolific author and speaker. Phyllis Curott, a pioneering attorney and Elder Wiccan priestess, continues to be a strong voice in the community, advocating for religious freedom and spiritual empowerment. The Hoodwitch, Bri Luna, offers a chic, modern take on witchcraft that resonates with her audience while maintaining a deep respect for traditional practices. Michael Herkes, known as the Glam Witch, brings a fresh, vibrant perspective to the craft with his emphasis on glamor and self-empowerment. Christian Day and his husband Brian Cain have been frontrunners of supporting the international occult community: together they host HexFest and the international online convention WitchCon, and they provide hubs in Salem and New Orleans and run a publishing company - as well as being initiated Alexandrian priests and welcoming Maxine Sanders (co-founder of Alexandrian Wicca) to the USA.

These figures, along with countless new voices emerging on platforms like TikTok and Instagram, showcase the diversity and inclusivity that define modern witchcraft. Despite their differences, they all share a deep respect for the sacredness of nature and a commitment to personal empowerment and spiritual growth. This vibrant community continues to evolve, reflecting the multifaceted nature of the craft itself.

When negativity arises about witchcraft on social media, especially on platforms like TikTok I choose not to let it infiltrate my spirit. Experience flows where attention goes, so I'm intentional about where I place mine. Rather than engaging with or absorbing bitterness, I observe it, acknowledge it, and then release it, allowing it to pass by like a shadow. This practice strengthens my mental and spiritual health, helping me stay focused on my path with peace and resilience.

WHAT WITCHES BELIEVE

There are a few basic ideologies that all witches share.

Nature is sacred

Modern witches, though often living busy urban lives, find nature divinely empowered - we acknowledge and respect as sacred the spirit within all things, animate and inanimate. We consider it our duty to repair, heal, and conserve the environment and all life on this planet as constructively as we can.

I remember having a profound experience of the "(w)holiness" of nature when I was touring with my old band Def FX through the lush hinterland of northern New South Wales. After three weeks on the road, I was totally toxic - my lungs were caked with smoke from the gigs, and I felt buried in the metal cesspool on wheels that was our Tarago van speeding down the highway. My body was trapped, but my gaze followed the gentle swells and jutting peaks of the surrounding mountain range, and suddenly I felt something in me shift. Instead of looking at the mountains, I became them. My muscles were heavy, damp earth, my blood was trickling streams, and my breath was the wind that spiraled in and out of the trees. I was a "Lady of the Mountain" and utterly present in this reality.

I had a deep sense of patience and eternity and an intense underlying sensation of growing - slowly but so powerfully that it was almost violent. I could feel each blade of grass jutting out of my skin; my bones became the gnarled roots of trees easing themselves in and out of the earth that was me. I was as close to knowing heaven as I'd ever been in my life at that point - a nirvanic sense of bliss, all the more for the sensation of my free, blissed-out spirit being juxtaposed with the grotty reality my physical body was in. I was overwhelmed by how utterly magnificent nature is.

When I think of nature as sacred, I think of it from a Darwinian perspective - that as a species we are evolved of this biosphere and we are intimately connected to all life forms upon it: the stuff of oceans, mountains, stars, animals, and trees are all within us. When I consciously connect with this, I know I can align my spirit with the spirit of all living things. After that first experience, I can now make my physical sense of self 'shift' to accommodate this alignment when I am doing ritual.

There is a Goddess and a God

One of the most empowering aspects of witchcraft today remains our reverence for the Goddess, the feminine face of divinity that celebrates balance, sensuality, and nurturance. This isn't just appealing to women - men are drawn to her as well, often discovering the freedom to explore the feminine within themselves, an aspect long suppressed by patriarchal structures. Many of us honor the Goddess as the triple-faced deity of the moon - maiden, mother, and crone - whose wisdom and power echo through the moon's phases, waxing, full, and waning.

I have a deep connection with the image of the Great Earth Mother, Gaia. On my first altar, I placed a green statue of Gaia herself, her face serene, pregnant belly painted with our blue planet

- a piece aptly named *The Millennial Gaia*, crafted by my friend Oberon Zell and his late wife, Morning Glory of Mythic Images, reminding me of the grounded, nurturing spirit at the core of witchcraft's living practices.

The God of witchcraft, often honored as the Horned Lord of the Forests, embodies the primal, pulsing life force within nature. He is a timeless presence, a spirit of wild freedom and fertility, with many names - Pan, Cernunnos, the Green Man - and countless forms. He stands as the guardian of the earth's living cycles, from seed to sprout to towering tree, reminding us of the raw, untamed energy that courses through all living things. Popular imagery may still picture him as part man, part beast - with a powerful torso, mischievous glint in his eyes, and cloven-hoofed legs - but his essence is far greater than any single depiction. He is the fire in the forest, the pulse in the soil, and the spark that calls us back to our own wildness.

Living in Egypt, I've been profoundly aware of their presence within the iconic structures of this magnificent land, where human civilization as we know it was born. I have experienced conscious, lucid interactions with these ancient gods and goddesses, and they impart a clear message: "The gods are not to be called upon and demanded of! We are to be venerated, and then we decide what you need." This sacred reciprocity, which requires respect and honor, is at the heart of communion with the divine and has reshaped my practice, underscoring that reverence must always be at the foundation of true connection.

Witches understand the God and Goddess not as beings separate from us, but as energies deeply intertwined with our own spirits. They are within us, of us, and we are of them - a dynamic exchange that resonates both internally and externally. We each carry aspects of the gods and goddesses within, reflecting their qualities in our lives and choices. In this way, every witch has the potential to be a priestess or priest, not as a hierarchy but as a testament to experience, dedication, and personal evolution in the craft.

Yet, just as witchcraft respects personal agency, it also embraces the fluidity of belief. Some of us view the deities as independent presences beyond our individual consciousness - living, breathing energies that exist in their own right. Others may see them as archetypes or projected energies, reflections of our collective psyche or inner world. Each perspective is equally valid, for our connection to the divine is ultimately a personal journey. Whether we approach the God/dess as a symbol or a sacred ally, the magick lies in honoring that presence, within and without, as a force of wisdom, power, and transformation.

Reincarnation and the cycle of life

Most witches believe in reincarnation - the journey of the soul through various lives and physical forms, learning, growing, and understanding its divine purpose. My rational scientific brain struggles with the notion of humans evolving toward some ideal of perfection. What does "good" or "perfect" truly mean in a world so complex and fraught with challenges?

As I revisit these thoughts, wars are breaking out and being fought across the world underscoring the heartbreaking reality of conflict. The devastation affects both soldiers and civilians, with lives disrupted and futures uncertain. Many of us inherently feel that war and killing are wrong. Yet, for those involved - whether soldiers fighting under the banner of duty or civilians caught in the crossfire - the immediacy of survival often overshadows broader ethical considerations. They are driven by a sense of necessity, loyalty, and sometimes a deep conviction that they are protecting their people and land.

Nature mirrors our conflicts. Just as wars erupt among nations, so too do they occur in the natural world. I recall watching an invasive lantana bush overtake an indigenous boronia in my parents' backyard. At first, I wondered - was it wrong? But nature doesn't operate on human moral codes. It exists by different laws: survival, adaptation, dominance, and transformation.

Yet the lantana was battling not by nature's original design, but because humans had introduced it. When we interfere with nature's innate intelligence, we often create further conflict. These disruptions are not just environmental - they're a reflection of our own displacement as a species. Witchcraft, by virtue of honoring nature's sacred order, seeks to restore balance. It calls us back to a deeper listening, a reverence for cycles we didn't invent but are part of.

The cycles of death, destruction, and decay are as natural as birth, growth, and renewal. Within them, we find both conflict and harmony - forces that coexist. Unlike human wars, which are often fueled by greed and moral distortion, nature offers a different kind of power. There is an elegance in its interdependence, a gentle harmony in its wild order. The flower opens. The bee comes. Nectar is shared, pollen is carried, life continues.

There is a blueprint here for us: co-creative harmony - a power that regenerates rather than dominates. If we choose to see it, nature can be our greatest teacher - offering a path not of conquest, but of communion.

In our quest for understanding, we might find solace in the belief that all experiences, even the painful and chaotic ones, contribute to the soul's evolution. Whether in the macrocosm of nature or the microcosm of human society, every event, every life, and every conflict has its place in the grand scheme of things. As witches, we seek to navigate these complexities with compassion, wisdom, and a deep reverence for the interconnectedness of all beings.

Rather than reincarnation being a spiritual ladder to perfection, I choose to relate to it as more a process of cellular genetic inherited memory. In my genes is the DNA of my ancestors, and their lives and experiences sometimes awaken in me when I meditate or dream deeply. Essentially, my consciousness unravels their existence from the double spiral helix within me, and I can relive their experiences as a part of me. I wrote at length about this in my first book, *Witch: a Personal Journey*, in the "Déjà Vu" chapter, and revisited the topic 30 years later in my manifesto *The Art of Witch*. It still amazes me that I once had recurrent regressive dream therapy that revealed to me a previous life as a Jewish child living in northern Europe during the Second World War and who was put to death in a gas chamber. What makes this extraordinary is that when I later searched for my biological parents in my late twenties, I found that my father was Jewish, born in Hungary, and I had relatives who had been imprisoned in German prisoner of war camps.

What comes after life? Death, and then life anew. The energy within us transitions and continues. The idea of being interred beneath a tree, contributing to its growth and becoming part of its life cycle, is comforting. The Celts traditionally planted sacred trees like oak, ash, and elder on graves, a practice I might consider in my will. However, I feel more inclined toward cremation, with this body's ashes scattered at sea or released to the winds from a mountaintop.

In my 30 years of dedicated practice, including divination, spirit channeling, and other extraordinary phenomena beyond mainstream experiences, I've come to understand that the veils between worlds are remarkably thin. When we set aside our ego and self-identity, we can become vessels for not only our primary spirit but also for other spirits needing to communicate. In my case, these spirits often wish to convey messages to my clients or friends, with whom they share a powerful emotional bond. My primary skill in facilitating this process lies in my ability to step aside from my own ego and identity, allowing information, conversations, observations, and comments to flow through unimpeded.

I have no doubt about the existence of the spirit realm. It doesn't operate within the same time or plane of existence as our physical form, but it coexists with us at all times. My life as a witch has enabled me to embrace this reality, finding comfort and contentment in the continuous presence of the spirit world.

Some witches embrace the concept of Summerland - a realm often envisioned as a peaceful, witchy afterlife akin to the Christian idea of Heaven, yet with fewer stringent entry requirements. However, I don't rely on the promise of an afterlife to find meaning in this life. Instead, I believe the moments immediately following death are pivotal. Our brain, continuing to function briefly after the heart ceases, offers us a unique window to contemplate our transition.

During this twilight phase, I speculate that our consciousness might influence our journey to the next plane of existence. It could act as a kind of slingshot, propelling us into a new realm or reality. While I'm not eager to hasten the end, I am curious and even eager to experience the mystery of dying. I anticipate it will be an extraordinary moment, one that offers a profound exploration of existence beyond our physical form.

In embracing the uncertainty and potential of what comes next, I find a deep sense of comfort and curiosity. My life as a witch has taught me that the spiritual and physical worlds are intimately connected, and the journey between them, however unknown, is a continuation of our soul's quest for understanding and growth.

Cœur
fidèle

THE LAWS OF WITCHCRAFT

While all laws are made to be broken - and many are subjective depending on the situation - most witches still choose to live by these ones.

Do what you will as long as you harm none.

The first law is straightforward: do not use your craft to harm others. This principle underscores the ethical responsibility inherent in practicing witchcraft.

Do what you will but do not interfere with another's free will.

The second law emphasizes the importance of consent. In fact, it could be renamed in these modern times: consent is crucial. Never perform magick on another person without their explicit permission, even for well-meaning intentions like healing spells. If obtaining consent is impossible, be prepared to accept the consequences of your actions, whether positive or negative.

MAGICKAL INTEGRITY IN HEALING SPELLS

Sometimes people must walk through pain to find their power. Intervening too directly - without consent - can rob a person of vital growth. Instead, craft your healing spells to offer support, not control. Call in divine assistance, strength, or clarity only if it serves their highest good and harms none. With the right wording, your magick becomes not an imposition but an offering.

As you send out so returns threefold.

The third law, often misunderstood, does not simply mean that good deeds bring good rewards and bad deeds bring bad repercussions threefold. It is a reminder to be aware of and take responsibility for your actions. A wise witch never intentionally causes harm, but even when doing good, it should be done unconditionally, honoring the nurturing and regenerative aspects of the craft.

Magick is the art of creating change with will.

A witch's strength lies in their will. I often tell newcomers that one key sign of being a witch is the strength of their will. Developing and training our will is our greatest discipline. With a strong will, supplemented by carefully chosen crystals, herbs, incantations, and the full moon, a witch can cast spells to manifest their desires effectively.

But I would also offer, as our craft has evolved and as I have expounded in my recent manifesto *The Art of Witch* . . . that "will" now becomes the foundation of the word "willing" - willing to be of service; willing to be a conduit, a channel of divine healing and sustenance for a weary, drained human world. It is true to say that a witch's greatest show of power is not determined by what she can get with her magick . . . but what she can *give*.

All acts of love and pleasure are sacred to the Goddess.

In witchcraft, sex can be sacred - but it is not the only path to sacredness. The energy of orgasm may be consciously offered to the universe for healing, manifestation, or growth in the same way as prayer, meditation, or ritual devotion. For some witches, love-making is a way to honor the land and connect deeply with the cycles of nature, while others choose celibacy or channel their power through different sacred practices. There is no one-size-fits-all path. What matters is the intention behind the act, and the awareness of the energy being raised and directed. Whether through ecstatic pleasure, stillness, or quiet contemplation, all sincere acts of connection can be offerings to the divine.

I remember when I first heard the phrase "All acts of love and pleasure are sacred to the Goddess." It kind of blew my mind - and honestly, it challenged a lot of the guilt I'd been carrying from my Catholic upbringing. The idea that I could actually enjoy my body, that sex wasn't something shameful or sinful but something divine? That was radical. Witchcraft gave me a way to unlearn all the repression and start feeling at home in my skin. Over time, I realized pleasure isn't something to be hidden or judged - it's something to be honored. And not just sexual pleasure, but joy, laughter, affection, connection. All of it. That's what makes this path so healing.

In perfect love and perfect trust.

This phrase is a cornerstone of many witches' practices, reflecting peace and harmony with all things. It is a declaration of dedication to the universal forces of magick.

With harm to none and for the good of all.

Often said at the end of spells and rituals, this reaffirmation aligns with the primary witch's law: "Do what you will as long as you harm none." This principle ensures that actions are aimed at the greater good, anchoring efforts in positivity, establishment of co-creative balance, and dynamic evolution.

Celebrate all expressions of the human spirit.

Witches respect all religions, recognizing that different paths aim to achieve happiness, purpose, and meaning. We educate ourselves about various religions to express respect and tolerance intelligently.

Coming out of the broom closet.

Despite increased acceptance, misconceptions about witchcraft persist. Modern witches are equipped to address these misunderstandings with concise and enlightened explanations. For instance, one might explain that belief in the devil is a Christian concept, not applicable to witches, whose roots lie in ancient pagan traditions.

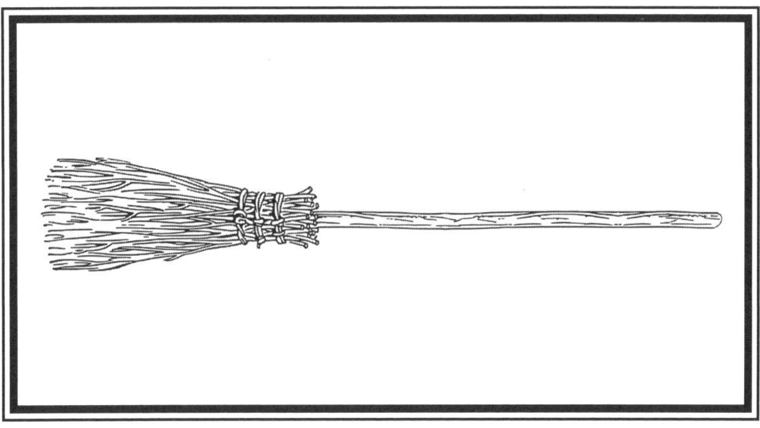

It's all good.

Witches celebrate all positive expressions of the human spirit, including different religions. We believe in personal empowerment through responsible living, harmony with the environment, and respect for all living things. This philosophy guides us in educating others and dispelling myths about witchcraft.

By following these principles, witches honor the essence of their craft, fostering a positive and ethical practice that aligns with the greater good.

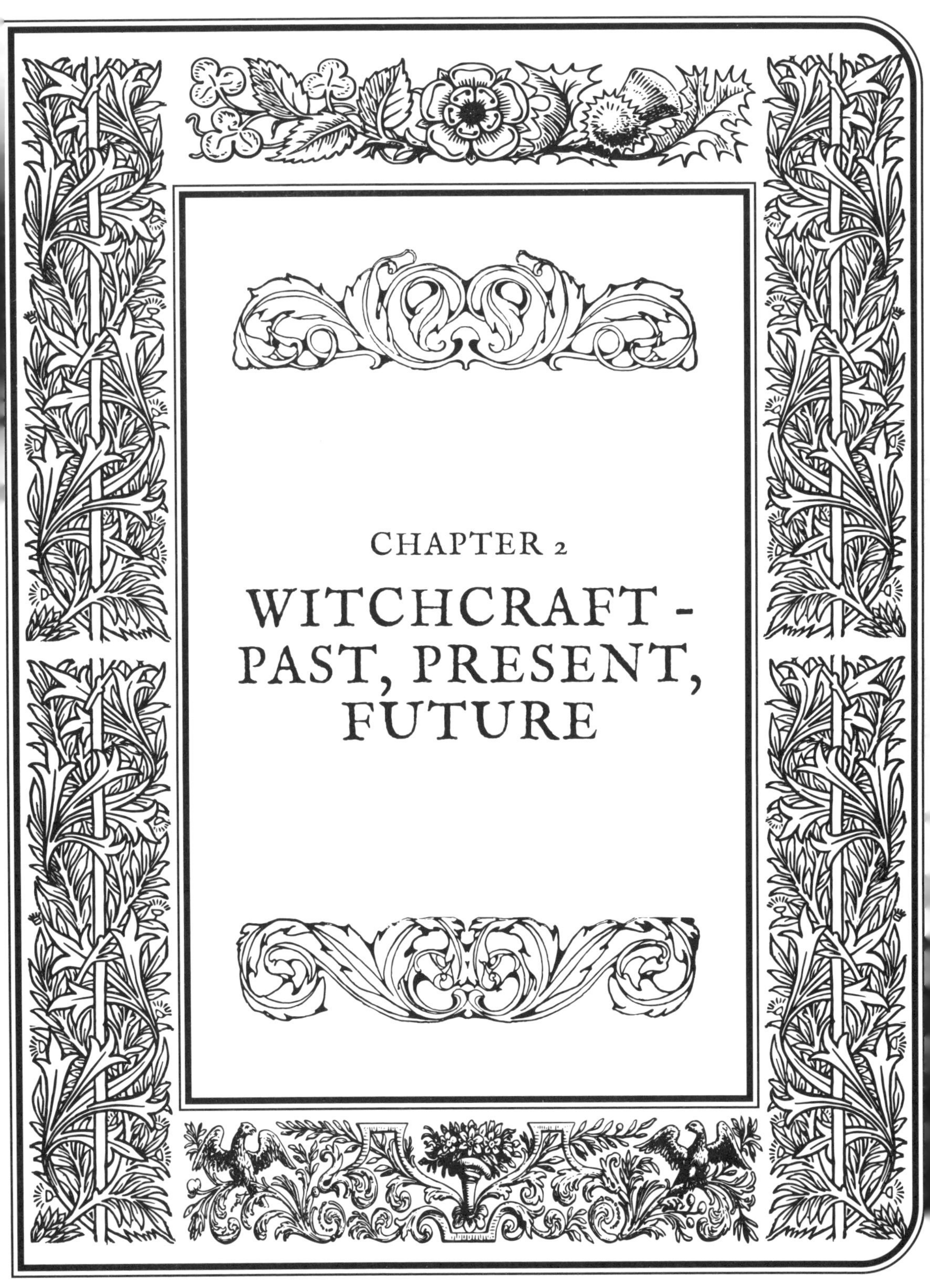

CHAPTER 2

WITCHCRAFT - PAST, PRESENT, FUTURE

The herstory of the craft is a fascinating amalgam of ever-evolving activities and selective memories, responding to the needs of the people and planet in the eternal present moment of now.

PAST

I wrote extensively about the herstory of witchcraft in my first two books, *Witch: a Personal Journey* and *Witch: a Magickal Year*, but here is some material I haven't commented on specifically before, along with fresh projections on where Wicca/witchcraft is headed now.

Witchcraft continues to flourish and evolve, firmly established as one of the fastest-growing spiritual paths in Australia and across the Western world. As far back as the 2001 Australian Census, Wicca and paganism were identified among the most rapidly expanding religious affiliations - and more than two decades later, this trend has not only continued but intensified.

This modern resurgence blends traditional practices with contemporary influences, offering an alternative to institutional religion. Many are drawn to witchcraft's focus on personal experience, nature-based spirituality, and inclusive ethos. It resonates deeply with those who identify as "spiritual but not religious" - in other words, those who seek meaning, empowerment, and connection beyond dogma.

The rise of online platforms like TikTok and Instagram have further accelerated witchcraft's popularity, especially among younger generations. These digital spaces have become fertile ground for sharing rituals, spells, and magickal insight, building a sense of global community and creative expression.

Dr. Helen A. Berger, a leading sociologist of religion and contemporary paganism, has explored these trends in her 2023 research published through Brandeis University. Her work highlights how the modern witchcraft movement continues to expand in response to shifting cultural values, including environmental awareness, gender equity, and spiritual autonomy. Witchcraft today is a living, adaptable path - rooted in the old ways, yet speaking powerfully to the needs of the present.

Modern Wicca and witchcraft draw their roots from the earth-honoring spiritual traditions of pre-Christian Europe, including the ritual-rich cultures of the Celts and the nature-revering beliefs of the Germanic and Norse peoples, the mystery traditions of ancient Greece and Rome, and later in the speculative religious science of the Gnostics and the Zoroastrians.

As Christianity gradually exerted its dominance throughout the early part of the last millennium, it declared all other faiths and practices heretical and worthy of persecution. This culminated in the Inquisitions of the medieval and early modern eras. In 1484, Pope Innocent VIII issued the papal bull recognizing and criminalizing witchcraft, which stepped up the Roman Catholic Church's war against so-called witches. The bull appeared two years later as a preface to the *Malleus Maleficarum* (*Hammer of the Witches*), a guide to witch hunting. Historians disagree over the number tortured and killed as "witches" over the next 400 years, with figures ranging from 40,000 to 6 million; regardless of the exact number, it was far too many.

The Church's concept of witchcraft relied on superstition and hysterical fear. Accusations became tools for amassing power and wealth, rarely involving legitimate proof of wrongdoing. Charges against "witches" often included fantastical claims like holding Black Masses with the Devil or transforming into animals. These charges were also direct attacks on women, as the *Malleus Maleficarum* attributed witch powers to "carnal lust" and female sexuality.

During this period, pagan ways went underground. Some modern witches believe Wicca, the craft of the wise, was practiced in secret and resurfaced in the mid-20th century with initiates like Gerald Gardner and Doreen Valiente. They reinstated the legitimacy and acceptance of the craft by making information available to a broader audience. Gardner sourced ritual structure and imagery from Celtic traditions, Masonic ritual, Samuel Mathers and Florence Farr's Hermetic Order of the Golden Dawn, Aleister Crowley's occult practices, Gnostic and Rosicrucian beliefs, and shamanic practices.

In 1951, the anti-witchcraft laws of England were repealed. Gardner and Valiente's works captured the public's imagination, spearheading a revival of the Old Ways. In the 1960s and 1970s, Alex and Maxine Sanders forged their tradition, incorporating Kabbalah and ceremonial magick. Public witches like Sybil Leek further demystified witchcraft.

The New Age explosion of the 1980s provided more room for witchcraft. Influential writers and witches like Starhawk, Z. Budapest, Raymond Buckland, and Scott Cunningham made information more accessible.

The rise of the 1990s witch

In the 1990s, witchcraft experienced a cultural and spiritual renaissance, stepping boldly into the mainstream through a wave of popular media and a growing body of published works that presented witches as powerful, complex, and relatable. TV shows like *Buffy the Vampire Slayer*, *Charmed*, and *Sabrina the Teenage Witch* brought magickal women into living rooms across the world, while films like *The Craft*, *Practical Magic*, and *Hocus Pocus* sparked imaginations and ignited an appetite for real-life spellcraft.

This was also the era when real witches began stepping into the public eye. I was appearing regularly across media in Australia, the UK, and the USA, becoming one of the most recognizable public faces of modern witchcraft. My first books, published post-1998, became bestsellers - offering grounded, experiential teachings from my own practice, and making the craft accessible to a whole new generation of seekers.

At the same time, *WitchCraft Magazine* launched in Australia - a monthly publication by a mainstream media company. Its founding editor, Lucy Cavendish, had previously worked on the magazine *Australian Women's Forum* and would go on to become one of the country's most respected authors and spokespeople for the craft. *WitchCraft Magazine*'s very existence was a sign of the times: witchcraft was no longer hidden - it was being explored openly, seriously, and with beauty and respect.

Other powerful voices were rising too, such as American lawyer and Wiccan priestess Phyllis Curott, whose groundbreaking memoir *Book of Shadows* introduced countless readers to the inner world of witchcraft as both spiritual path and personal empowerment.

The 1990s marked a turning point - the word "witch" was being reclaimed with pride. What had once been feared or misunderstood was now being lived out loud, laying the foundation for the vibrant, inclusive, and globally connected magickal communities of today.

PRESENT

The number of individuals identifying as witches has risen dramatically. In the United States, estimates suggest that there are 1-1.5 million people practicing Wicca or paganism, a significant increase from the estimated 8,000 Wiccans in 1990. This growth reflects a broader trend of individuals seeking spiritual paths that resonate with personal beliefs and experiences.

Witchcraft has evolved significantly over the past few decades, gaining both maturity and legitimacy. Globally, anti-witchcraft laws have been repealed, and Wicca is now recognized as a religion with legal tax-exempt status in several countries. In Australia, the Discrimination Act of 1991 protected against religious discrimination but it was not until 2013 that witchcraft was finally decriminalized across all of Australia.

Today, witches embrace technology, using the internet to learn, share, and connect. We see it as our duty to heal the earth, approaching our magick with a scientific slant and embracing concepts like quantum physics. Our path is eclectic, intertwining various traditions.

The integration of technology has further facilitated the spread and acceptance of witchcraft practices. Online platforms and social media have allowed practitioners to connect, share knowledge, and build communities, contributing to the growing visibility and normalization of witchcraft in the modern world.

As we continue to embrace and adapt to these changes, the practice of witchcraft remains a dynamic and evolving spiritual path, reflecting the diverse experiences and beliefs of its practitioners worldwide.

I am currently living in Egypt, deeply immersed in exploring the spiritual practices and traditions of the ancient Egyptians. Here, I understand how mystics of the late 1800s, like Samuel Mathers and Florence Farr, were inspired to create the Order of the Golden Dawn as the British Museum began displaying extraordinary

Egyptian artifacts that had recently been unearthed. Mathers, Farr, and their followers would commune with these artifacts, receiving messages from a world beyond imagining. These proud treasures were scoured from the hot dry desert of Egypt by the likes of Howard Carter and other colonials and brought the fire of spiritual inspiration with them to cloudy cold England.

Aleister Crowley, an influential English occultist, ceremonial magickian, poet, early member of the Golden Dawn, and ultimately founder of the religion of Thelema, was deeply aligned with ancient Egypt. During his time in Cairo with his wife Rose, he spent a night inside the Great Pyramid of Giza and had a profound experience of energy, intention, light, and electricity. This profoundly influenced his magickal practices, leading him to incorporate Egyptian deities, symbols, and rituals into his Thelemic teachings, most notably through his reception of *The Book of the Law* during his stay in Cairo.

Crowley stated that the book was dictated to him by a supernatural entity named Aiwass over three days in April 1904 in Cairo. This text forms the cornerstone of Crowley's spiritual philosophy, Thelema.

W. B. Yeats, the celebrated Irish poet and Nobel laureate, was also deeply immersed in the esoteric world of the Golden Dawn. His involvement significantly influenced his poetic work, infusing it with mystical and symbolic elements. Yeats was particularly fascinated with ancient Egypt, a culture revered within the Order for its profound spiritual knowledge and magickal practices. This fascination is evident in his poetry and plays, where he often alluded to Egyptian gods, symbols, and themes of eternal life and transformation, reflecting his belief in the interconnectedness of all spiritual traditions and his quest for deeper metaphysical truths.

And it is the forementioned spiritual explorers who formed the cornerstones for what Gerald Gardner brought forth with a new religion . . .

Gardner, often regarded as the father of modern Wicca, had a significant but indirect connection with the Order of the Golden Dawn. While Gardner was not a member of the Golden Dawn himself, he was heavily influenced by it. Gardner was initiated into the New Forest Coven in the late 1930s, and, through this group, he was introduced to various occult practices and traditions.

The New Forest Coven, and other early Wiccan groups, were influenced by the esoteric knowledge and rituals of the Golden Dawn, which was founded by Samuel Liddell MacGregor Mathers and other prominent occultists in the late 19th century. The Golden Dawn was known for its extensive system of magickal training and ceremonial rituals, many of which drew upon ancient Egyptian, Hermetic, and Kabbalistic traditions.

Gerald Gardner's development of Wicca incorporated elements from these traditions, blended with folklore, Western esotericism, and his own innovations. The influence of the Golden Dawn can be seen in the structure of Wiccan rituals, the use of ceremonial tools, and the emphasis on the balance of masculine and feminine energies, which parallels the Golden Dawn's own magickal framework.

In essence, while Gerald Gardner was not directly affiliated with the Order of the Golden Dawn, the legacy of the Golden Dawn's teachings significantly shaped the formation and practices of modern Wicca . . . which of course is modern witchcraft, and all its 1,000 unfolding petals.

FUTURE

Where is witchcraft headed? It will continue to bring together more voices, celebrating diversity and inclusiveness. As global borders blur, the indigenous spiritual paths of our planet merge, and our craft is practiced by anyone in the human genetic mixing pot.

Witchcraft's insistence on individual empowerment is our strength. The fact that Wicca will never be dominated by one book, voice, or vision guarantees its relevance and survival. I think witchcraft is the one of the smartest spiritual paths on the planet in this respect. It truly is an egalitarian, positively evolved, and empowered expression of the human spirit.

With the digital explosion, as life becomes more virtual, this evolution could actually benefit the natural world. The more lightly we tread on the Great Mother, the better. Decentralized communities, digital nomads, and a return to simpler, cleaner living - assisted by the conveniences of digital communication - can create a fertile, positive environment for future witchcraft.

This includes the awareness and practice of sustainable foraging and fossicking, ethical crystal sourcing, and using local substitutions for rare or non-local ingredients in spells and rituals. This not only lessens the air traffic carbon footprint but also reduces the endless radiation from shipped goods. Minimizing reliance on corporate behemoths like online shopping services is essential.

The future of witchcraft embraces technology to foster connection and learning while honoring and protecting our planet. By integrating digital advancements with sustainable practices, we can ensure that our craft remains a powerful, earth-centered, and transformative path for generations to come.

CONJURING A RELIGION

Some people have issues with the possibility of witchcraft being "fabricated" as a fantastical mix of wishful thinking and fairy tales. But aren't all religions/spiritual paths fabricated at some point? Contemporary witchcraft may not have an unbroken connection to the most ancient traditions of European magick, as some earlier Wiccan books claimed, but this doesn't negate the path any more than Darwin's Genesis-debunking theory of evolution stopped Christianity. It is natural and inevitable that religions and spiritual practices emerge in ways that reflect the cultural, social, and spiritual evolution of our species for as long as we continue to inhabit this planet.

Reflecting now, I find it interesting to analyze my childhood and see how many practices of witchcraft I intuitively incorporated into my life before I had read any book on witchcraft. I always experienced nature as magickal from as early as I can remember.

I used to make wishes by floating leaves on the river and watching them carried away to come true. I left offerings for the flower spirits on a flat rock at the edge of the cliff in front of our house. I see these acts as akin to the positive spells and nature-honoring rituals of my later years as an educated witch. I did not perform these actions to harm, control, or mislead but to emphasize and enjoy my feelings of connectedness with the miraculous natural world around me.

I would play in the bush for hours; wandering along the tracks I would pick bush flowers, always thanking the plant and leaving an offering of some sort - a feather, a pretty pebble, or a kiss. I would stare at the flowers, enjoying their shape, texture, and color for so long that often a mist would form around them; perhaps it was their auras that my vision distinguished. I would sneak out of the house and sit by the river, drunk with the beauty of the sunlight dancing on the water as it flushed over my toes, cold and pure. My fingers would touch the sparkles in the granite rock that I sat on, and I would feel shivers of electricity shimmer into my hands as I absorbed the energy of the ancient stone.

In my later years, when I started to read books on paganism and witchcraft, my mind often returned to those pure, sacred moments of my childhood. I realized I had been a witch all along.

CHAPTER 3

COVENCRAFTING

There are numerous ways to form a coven. Traditional methods, often based on Gardnerian principles are widely encouraged in many books on the subject. However, as witchcraft evolves, a more fluid and less structured approach to coven creation is emerging, mirroring modern societal structures and the more contemporary, less gender-specific roles that individuals play.

Witchcraft today is about so much more than what you wear or the tools you use - it's a deeply personal spiritual practice that adapts to each individual's path. Popular images - like black hats, crystals, tarot cards, and cauldrons - have become iconic symbols that many associate with witchcraft, influenced by media, fashion, and social movements. Yet true witchcraft goes beyond these images. It's rooted in connection with nature, personal empowerment, and honoring the cycles of life and the divine.

Witches are as likely to be found in business suits as in flowing robes, practicing magick with intention and respect. This modern diversity reflects witchcraft's adaptability and the freedom it offers each practitioner to express their beliefs authentically, beyond any single look or trend.

To ensure that Wicca and witchcraft continue to grow and reflect humanity's evolving spiritual state, we must delve beneath the surface and examine the core beliefs and practices of witchcraft:

- Nature is a divine expression of the life force and is thus sacred and empowered.
- We are nature, intricately connected with the earth and all its living and non-living components.
- We are God/dess.
- Heaven is here on earth, and the greatest happiness, freedom, and peace are found in the present moment.

Witchcraft is a way of living as divine and empowered beings. Its tools, rituals, and ideas help us connect with and experience the witches' worldview: that heaven is now; that every expression of love and pleasure is sacred to the God/dess; and that death, destruction, and difficulty are natural and necessary parts of the cycle of life. Every human is "super-naturally" empowered to create the life they desire.

THE EVOLUTION OF ONLINE WITCHCRAFT

The growth of online witchcraft communities and the integration of digital tools have significantly expanded the reach and influence of modern magickal practices. So we see stats like over 20 billion views of WitchTok videos as of 2024; over 20 million Instagram posts with the hashtag #Witchcraft; and thousands of YouTube channels dedicated to witchcraft, with top influencers having millions of subscribers. There is also a rapidly growing virtual reality witchcraft community with immersive VR rituals and spellcasting, attracting tech-savvy witches. The infinitely diverse world of online witchcraft has transformed modern magickal practice to include the virtual realm, incorporating AI-enhanced appearances and spellcasting.

Meanwhile, publications like *The Wall Street Journal* and *The Conversation* have highlighted the economic impact of the now-mainstream interest in witchcraft, with the latter describing it as a multi-billion-dollar industry.

The integration of technology in witchcraft practices reflects a broader trend of digitalization in spiritual and religious practices, enhancing accessibility and engagement for practitioners around the globe. As the practice continues to evolve, the digital realm offers new opportunities for community building, learning, and innovation in the magickal arts.

When I originally came out of the broom closet and wrote my first book, almost 30 years ago, there was no internet, no social media; it was a solitary practice, truly occult, and the effort it took to find a coven and practice with others was devoutly sincere and took months . . . sometimes years.

While the digital world offers us new opportunities to expand our reach, practice and knowledge, I still know with absolute clarity that the natural world is the true source of our power, and that our place within it is one of the ways the divine expresses itself . . . in this case, in human form. Just as many religions speak of humanity being made in the image of the divine, we, as witches, understand ourselves as living embodiments of that sacred force - one expression among many, but no less meaningful. Our craft is a practice of remembering this truth and honoring it through direct relationship with nature. That relationship can't be replicated or replaced by the digital world. If it is, then what's being practiced is no longer witchcraft. It's something else entirely.

Covencrafting seeks to create an orb of collective consciousness, a presence that prevails beyond the physical. It is an offering, a gift, to the magickal world. The essence of a coven lies not just in the rituals and spells, but in the unity of spirits, the convergence of energies, and the profound connection that transcends time and space.

When we gather, whether in a sacred grove under the full moon or in a cozy living room around a flickering candle, we weave our individual energies into a tapestry of collective power. This is the heart of covencrafting - a sacred space where our combined intentions amplify our magick, where our shared experiences deepen our understanding, and where our united spirits touch the divine.

In this sacred circle, we are reminded of our place in the cosmos. We see our reflection in the starry skies and feel the ancient pulse of the earth beneath our feet. The magick we create together is not confined to the here and now; it echoes through the ages, a timeless testament to our collective will and vision.

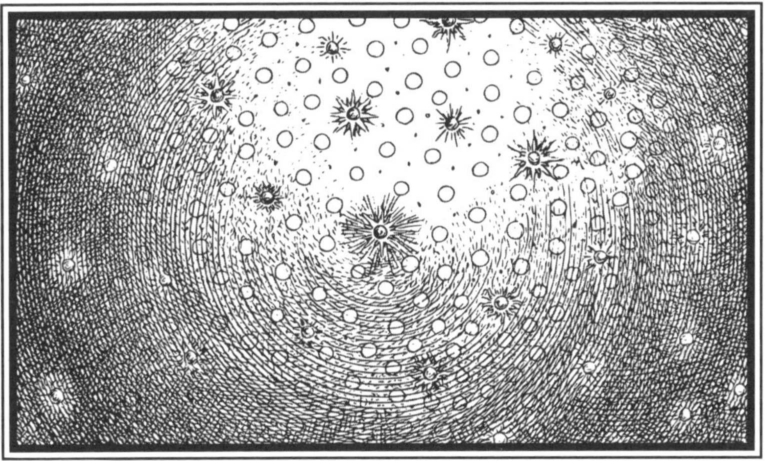

Our spirits, unbound by the physical, dance in the ether, creating ripples that shape the fabric of reality. This is the true power of a coven - a sanctuary of souls that harnesses the infinite potential of the human spirit. Each gathering, each ritual, each shared moment is an offering to the magickal world, a beacon of light in the darkness, a testament to the enduring power of unity.

As we walk this path together, let us honor the divine spark within each of us. Let us celebrate our connection to the natural world, our shared humanity, and our collective journey. This book is not just a guide; it is a celebration of the magick that lies within and around us, a call to embrace our power, and a reminder that in the sacred circle of the coven, we are never alone.

A modern coven that I propose in this book differs significantly from traditional covens of Gardnerian and Alexandrian witchcraft in several key aspects.

STRUCTURE AND FLEXIBILITY

Traditional covens:

- **Hierarchy and initiation:** Gardnerian and Alexandrian covens follow a structured hierarchy with clearly defined roles such as high priestess and high priest and various degrees of initiation. Initiation rituals are formal and often require a lengthy period of study and apprenticeship.
- **Strict adherence to tradition:** These covens adhere closely to established rituals, practices, and coven-specific teachings passed down through generations.

Modern covens:

- **Shared leadership:** Emphasize shared leadership and collaborative decision-making processes. Roles within the coven may be more fluid, with leadership rotating or shared among members.
- **Flexibility and innovation:** Encourage innovation and adaptation of rituals and practices to suit the needs and beliefs of the group. There is a greater emphasis on personal expression and contemporary relevance.

INCLUSIVITY AND DIVERSITY

Traditional covens:

- **Gender roles:** Gardnerian and Alexandrian traditions often emphasize polarity between male and female energies, with specific roles for men and women within rituals.

- **Selective membership:** Membership may be more selective, requiring potential members to undergo extensive vetting and initiation processes.

Modern covens:

- **Gender inclusivity:** Embrace a more inclusive approach to gender, welcoming members of all gender identities and sexual orientations. Rituals may emphasize a spectrum of energies rather than strict male/female dichotomies.
- **Open membership:** More open and welcoming to newcomers, with fewer barriers to entry and an emphasis on inclusivity and community support.

FOCUS AND ACTIVITIES

Traditional covens:

- **Ritual and worship:** Strong focus on formal rituals, worship of specific deities, and adherence to the Wheel of the Year.
- **Esoteric knowledge:** Emphasis on the study and practice of esoteric knowledge, often with a strong emphasis on secrecy and the occult.

Modern covens:

- **Humanitarian and environmental focus:** Integrate humanitarian acts and environmental commitments into their practices. Activities might include community service, ecological conservation efforts, and advocacy for social justice.

- Practical magick and healing: Greater emphasis on practical magick, such as healing with herbs, modern divination techniques, and supportive rituals for members in crisis. Focus on using magick as a tool for personal and communal growth.
- Digital integration: Utilize digital platforms for communication, virtual rituals, and learning, reflecting the integration of technology in modern spiritual practices more broadly.

COMMUNITY AND CONNECTION

Traditional covens:

- Secrecy and privacy: Often maintain a level of secrecy about their practices and members to preserve the sanctity and privacy of the coven.
- Local focus: Primarily local, with gatherings and rituals conducted in person, fostering deep face-to-face connections.

Modern covens:

- Openness and sharing: More openness about their practices, often sharing rituals, experiences, and teachings through social media and public events.
- Global reach: Utilize online platforms to connect with members worldwide, allowing for a broader, more diverse community. Virtual gatherings and digital communication tools facilitate connection and collaboration across distances.

CORE BELIEFS AND EVOLUTION

Traditional covens:

- **Established doctrine:** Rooted in specific doctrines and teachings that are meticulously preserved and passed down.
- **Conservative evolution:** Changes and adaptations to practices are slow and often debated extensively within the community.

Modern covens:

- **Dynamic beliefs:** Embrace a dynamic and evolving set of beliefs that can adapt to contemporary issues and the needs of the members.
- **Rapid adaptation:** More willing to experiment and integrate new ideas, reflecting the fast-paced changes of the modern world.

Overall, modern covens focus on inclusivity, shared leadership, and practical applications of magick to address contemporary issues, while still honoring the core principles of witchcraft. They blend traditional practices with innovative approaches, fostering a supportive and adaptive spiritual community.

CHAPTER 4

PATH TO BELONGING

This book is for those who have been practicing their magick as solitaries and feel ready to connect with a group of like-minded individuals to deepen their craft. Over the years, I've had the opportunity to be initiated into traditional covens across different paths. After thoughtful reflection, I chose not to proceed. The demands of my life back then - band tours, book signings, and workshops, and more recently travel and location - make it challenging to commit to the regular rhythm of a coven. And sometimes, the chemistry just wasn't there.

I hold a deep respect for traditional covens, though I don't relate to the hierarchical attitude that some have. I believe anyone drawn to the craft should have the opportunity to experience it, but that also means coven members have the right to say no if someone isn't a good fit.

THE ECLECTIC COVEN

The type of coven that has gained widespread popularity - and which this book explores - is the eclectic coven. This is a gathering of witches with diverse levels of experience who come together in a structured yet flexible way, reminiscent of a traditional coven but without rigid hierarchies. Instead, the focus is on evolving and practicing magick collectively in an inclusive, adaptive manner.

An eclectic coven often centers around an experienced witch who guides and mentors a group of committed members. These covens meet for important occasions such as full moons (Esbats), Sabbats, and sometimes weekly during their formative stages to build a cohesive "covenworld."

COVENWORLD (NOUN)

A covenworld is the energetic realm created by a coven's unified intent, focus, and magick. Once formed, a covenworld becomes a living, dynamic force - anchored in the astral plane - that protects, empowers, and nourishes each member, even when they are apart. Like an invisible yet ever-present current, it continues to function as an extension of the coven's energy. A covenworld is not imagined - it is manifested by group meditation, visualization, ritual, and the love and trust that binds the circle. It is a world within the world, a sacred construct sustained by magick, will, and heart.

To ensure all members share a strong foundation, a formal education program - like a Witchcraft 101 course - can be incredibly helpful. This can resemble the traditional year-and-a-day initiation. Many excellent online resources are available to guide this process; I've included links on my website, fionahorne.com. Additionally, the "Witchcraft 101" chapter in this book offers an eight-week course as a practical starting point.

An eclectic coven may flourish for years, growing and evolving together, or it might dissolve sooner if challenges arise. A year-and-a-day commitment is recommended, as it allows for navigating obstacles as opportunities for growth and transformation.

This was the foundation of my first coven in Los Angeles over 20 years ago. Initially, I took on the role of "leader" due to my experience. In an eclectic coven, the "leader" is typically the one who initiates gatherings, writes or sources rituals, and delegates tasks among the group. It's less about authority and more about collaboration.

My coven sisters, Tri and Lupita, were equally integral to our practice. We all maintained personal shrines and shared responsibilities. Tri might write a heartfelt ode to the Goddess, Lupita might craft a ritual wish list or memorize an invocation, and one of them might coordinate logistics or gather specific tools - like black agate crystal "caves" and candles - needed for our rituals.

An eclectic coven may not necessarily suit the needs or goals of every group of witches who want to journey together. There are other coven structures that can be adapted to enhance the practices and experiences of new witches seeking to travel with others.

THE WORKING GROUP

A working group is an excellent starting point for newer witches and can serve as a precursor to forming a formal coven. It's less about elaborate rituals and more like a study group. You meet regularly - once a week or more - to discuss witchcraft, read together, and share personal experiences.

A great way to kick off a working group is by choosing a book to read. Each person reads a few chapters and makes notes, and then you gather to discuss insights and reflections. Over time, these shared learnings could become the foundation for a collective Book of Shadows if the group evolves into a formal coven.

THE TEEN WITCH COVEN

Teen witches often have a natural affinity for magick. When forming a teen coven, it's important to consider the dynamics of youth, such as limited life experience, potential insecurities, and power struggles. Leadership roles should be shared equally to avoid hierarchies, as most members will have similar levels of knowledge. The emphasis should remain on learning and mutual support.

SPECIALTY COVENS

These covens reflect the diverse identities and interests of their members. Some examples include:

★ SAME-SEX COVENS: Girl covens, boy covens, or gay covens often foster a strong sense of unity and shared experience.
★ MIXED-SEX COVENS: Girl-boy covens or gay-hetero covens can also thrive but may require careful boundaries to avoid distractions.

In any coven, it's essential to keep personal relationships separate from the group's magickal work. Witchcraft views sexual energy as sacred, and while it can enhance a coven, it can also complicate dynamics. Maintaining focus on spiritual and magickal growth ensures the group's success.

THE VIRTUAL COVEN

While this book emphasizes in-person gatherings for their potent humanistic, naturally empowered, and divinely aligned benefits, virtual covens are a viable alternative. Creating an online coven can be a powerful act of magick and connection - a way to weave shared purpose across time and space. But digital spaces demand a different kind of discernment. Mistakes are part of magick. They teach you to trust your gut, sharpen your perception, and take responsibility for your choices. And being a witch has never been about being protected from life - it's about being equipped to navigate it.

A coven, online or otherwise, should never be about hierarchy or fear - it should be about clarity, empowerment, and growth. Set your boundaries with confidence, not anxiety. Create your digital circle with the same raw spirit you'd bring to a moonlit grove - and don't be afraid to take a few risks. Magick was never meant to be tame.

Craft an online coven with intention, resilience, and shared purpose.

Creating sacred space online:

- ★ VIRTUAL ALTAR: Encourage members to set up personal altars at home and share them virtually.
- ★ TECH CHECK: Ensure everyone is comfortable with the technology and troubleshoot issues beforehand.

Nourishing community:

- ★ WELCOMING RITUAL: Start with a welcoming ritual, lighting candles together and setting intentions.
- ★ CHECK-IN: Allow members to share their feelings and significant events to build connection.

Empowerment and goal setting:

- ★ GUIDED MEDITATION: Lead a grounding and centering meditation.
- ★ EMPOWERMENT CIRCLE: Have members share recent achievements or strengths.
- ★ PERSONAL GOALS: Guide members to identify personal magickal goals and share them.

Collaborative support:

- ★ BRAINSTORMING: Offer ideas and resources to support one another's goals.
- ★ ASSIGNING ROLES: Encourage members to volunteer for tasks to support each other.

Magickal working:

- ★ Collective spell: Conduct a group spell or ritual aimed at empowering each member's goal.
- ★ Energy raising: Use drumming or chanting to raise energy collectively.

Reflection and commitment:

- ★ Sharing experiences: Discuss insights gained during the ritual.
- ★ Gratitude circle: End on a positive note with expressions of gratitude.
- ★ Action steps: Outline steps members will take toward their goals and pair up as accountability buddies.

Continuous connection:

- ★ Online platform: Maintain an active online space for updates and support.
- ★ Regular check-ins: Schedule regular virtual meetings to maintain momentum.

Avoiding pitfalls:

- ★ Verify identities: Use video calls and check social media profiles.
- ★ Background checks: Ask for references from reputable community members.
- ★ Probationary period: Implement a probationary period for new members.
- ★ Clear guidelines: Establish a code of conduct.
- ★ Trust intuition: Encourage members to trust their instincts and voice concerns.
- ★ Secure platforms: Use secure platforms and optimize privacy settings.
- ★ Anonymous reporting: Provide a way to report suspicious behavior.

By following these guidelines, an online coven can create a deep sense of community, personal empowerment, and effective magickal practice, mirroring the benefits of in-person gatherings while adapting to the digital realm.

FINDING A COVEN

Connecting with like-minded witches may seem daunting, but there are many ways to start. Visit local metaphysical shops, attend community events, or explore online forums and social media groups dedicated to witchcraft. Be cautious when meeting people in person - always prioritize safety and take someone with you if meeting for the first time.

Finding the right coven takes time. Keep an open mind, and don't expect perfection immediately. Over time, you'll discover a group that resonates with your energy and values.

JOINING VS. STAYING SOLITARY

Being a solitary practitioner is just as valid as joining a coven. Whether you choose to work alone or with a group, both paths offer unique rewards. A coven can enhance your practice by bringing collective energy and shared wisdom, but it's not a requirement to be a "real" witch.

If you're unsure about joining a coven, start with a casual working group or participate in open rituals. This way, you can explore group dynamics without making a long-term commitment.

Congratulations on beginning this journey. Whether you start with a working group or plunge into forming an eclectic or teen coven, there is much to explore and achieve when you team up with other witches.

CHAPTER 5

FROM CONNECTION TO COMMITMENT

Finding the right members for your coven can be anything from serendipitously easy to a significant challenge. Joining an existing coven? That can be even trickier. So where do you begin? Should you approach people directly? Whether you're starting a coven or seeking one to join, it's best to follow the principles of the witches' creed:

- ★ Know what you want: Decide if your goal is to create or join a coven.
- ★ Will it into being: Visualize and manifest the reality you seek.
- ★ Dare to believe: Trust that the universe will guide the right people to you.
- ★ Be silent: This is perhaps the most challenging step. Witches don't preach, nor do we seek to convert others. Authentic connections happen naturally.

You might be thinking, "But how do I find the right people?" a good rule of thumb is to aim for a group of at least three people, including yourself, with a maximum of 13. Smaller covens often work more harmoniously, especially when everyone is new to the experience.

To illustrate "Be silent," let me share an experience from my Hollywood days. I was invited to a party by a friend who knew actor Crispin Glover (Michael J. Fox's father in the 1985 classic film *Back to the Future*). It was a private affair with a few notable people from the occult scene, as Crispin is interested in the unusual and unexplained.

At the party, I was introduced to Crispin, who was very charming. As the night progressed, a cavalcade of stars arrived: Cameron Diaz, Kate Hudson, Drew Barrymore, Nicolas Cage, and Lisa Marie Presley, among others. It was turning into a surreal night, not only because of the celebrities but also because of Crispin's topsy-turvy Spanish castle with doorways halfway up the wall and staircases leading nowhere.

Never did I mention being a witch to engage these celebrities' interest and potentially boost my career. Using witchcraft for self-promotion is disempowering and undignified. Instead, I kept my mouth shut and let them come to me. If Nicolas Cage or Drew Barrymore ever approach me because they've seen my work, I'll happily chat about my craft.

And a couple of years later I ended up consulting on the remake of the classic witchcraft film *The Wicker Man*, produced by Nic's company.

When seeking coven members, it's best to let them come to you. You might read a book on witchcraft in a public space, creating an opportunity for someone curious to approach you. Alternatively, you could post a discreet message in a community group, social media platform, or online forum. Something like, "Looking to connect with others interested in witchcraft and Wicca in [your location]." Be mindful of your privacy - use a dedicated email or a private messaging app rather than sharing personal contact details. Stay open and let the universe guide the right people your way.

For an online coven, you can post your intentions in relevant groups or forums and wait for responses. However, while online connections are a great way to build community, there's a depth and energy to gathering in person that can't quite be replicated digitally. If possible, I recommend working with people face-to-face first, then using online tools as a supplementary way to stay connected.

One of the most effective ways to attract like-minded souls is to set your intention clearly and trust the process. The right energies will find you if you remain open and authentic.

And, of course, you can always do a spell . . .

SPELL FOR ATTRACTING COVEN MEMBERS

YOU WILL NEED:

- ★ ONE LARGE PIECE OF PAPER
- ★ COLORED PENCILS IN THE RAINBOW SPECTRUM: red, orange, yellow, green, blue, indigo, and violet
- ★ SALT

AN OBJECT FOR EACH ELEMENT:

- ★ AIR/EAST: incense
- ★ EARTH/SOUTH IN THE SOUTHERN HEMISPHERE, NORTH IN THE NORTHERN HEMISPHERE: crystal
- ★ WATER/WEST: bowl of water
- ★ FIRE/NORTH IN THE SOUTHERN HEMISPHERE, SOUTH IN THE NORTHERN HEMISPHERE: candle

INSTRUCTIONS:

1. Sprinkle salt in a circle large enough for you to sit inside. Place the elemental objects in the quarters they are aligned with (i.e., north, south, east, and west). Place the paper and pencils in the center; you may like to include a small table to lean on.
2. Take a few deep breaths and connect with the fact that you are in a sacred, empowered space. Using the red pencil, draw a circle in the center of the paper and then divide the circle into seven sections. Slowly start coloring in each section with a different color of the rainbow. This represents the harmonious diversity you seek for your coven. As you color, chant:

   Colors work your perfect power.
   Draw to me my ideal coven.

3. Color the circle methodically and neatly, being careful not to go over the lines with each color. When the circle is fully colored, lick the tip of your index finger and place it in the center of the paper. Forcefully say:

   I call those who are meant to be,
   Come from the shadows unto me.
   Me and I becomes now we,
   My coveners be here with me.

4. Stay for a moment in this space; visions of people may appear in your mind's eye. Note the details - perhaps hair or eye color - whatever you can pick up. Remember these so that you can recognize these kindred spirits when they cross your path.
5. To end the ritual, roll the paper up and place it on your personal altar in the quarter of earth with a crystal on top to anchor your visualization in reality. Sweep up the salt and put it in the bin, throwing a little over your left shoulder as you do this.

EGO AND THE CRAFT

Ego gets in the way of true power. People who boast about themselves and their craft in a self-aggrandizing way are not true witches. True witches don't need to prove anything to anyone other than themselves.

HOW TO KNOW IF SOMEONE'S A GOOD FIT

Finding the right people to work magick with can be a challenge. Ego clashes, insecurities, and even a lack of commitment might arise. But many who are drawn to the craft are prepared to confront these aspects of themselves, often with transformative results. Part of being in a coven is about recognizing and smoothing out those personal rough edges - yours and others'.

At first, everyone may seem perfectly aligned, but over time, differences can surface. I address this in detail in the chapter "The art of coven keeping," but there are a few simple ways to assess compatibility when meeting potential coven members or considering someone for your group.

Astrological compatibility

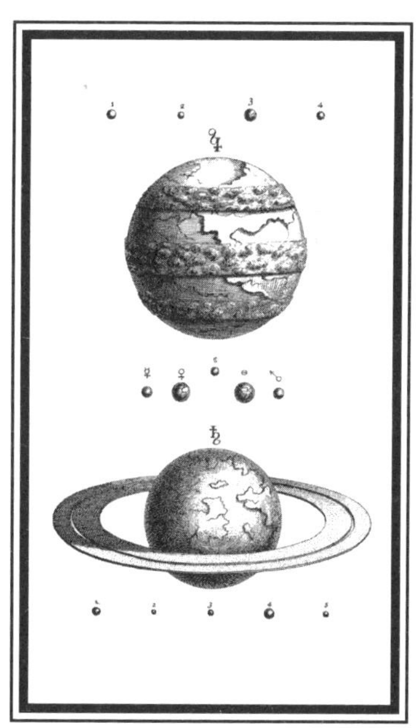

Understanding someone's sun (or star) sign can provide valuable insight into potential dynamics within the group. For example, I personally wouldn't thrive in a coven with two female Leos or two Scorpio males in close quarters - it's simply too much intensity for me. While it may seem extreme to exclude someone based on their astrological makeup, being aware of everyone's profiles can help you approach challenges with understanding and patience.

Astrology can also highlight compatibility within the group. Certain signs naturally balance each other's strengths and weaknesses, creating harmony. If you're curious, I recommend Linda Goodman's *Sun Signs* - a timeless classic and an excellent resource for understanding the interplay of personalities.

Gender dynamics

Same-sex covens often experience fewer distractions, as sexual tension is less likely to interfere with the work at hand. The sensual nature of witchcraft can act as an aphrodisiac, which might pull focus away from rituals and magickal intent. That said, this energy can also be a feature, not a bug. Witchcraft is inherently sensual, and all acts of love and pleasure are sacred to the Goddess.

For younger or less experienced groups, same-sex coven structures can provide a more focused environment for personal development and magick. Once the group is more established, introducing male-female polarities - or exploring other dynamics - can bring new layers of energy and meaning to the practice.

Ritual practices

In the early days of modern witchcraft, traditions like Gardnerian and Alexandrian covens placed a strong emphasis on fertility-focused rituals, often centering on the great rite (see the chapter "Sex as sacrament" for a description). Today, however, many covens explore magick in ways that are less rooted in overt sexuality, emphasizing diverse approaches to the craft.

While witchcraft remains deeply tied to the creative and generative forces of life, its expression is flexible. Gender-neutral or non-binary covens, for instance, often approach magick through innovative and inclusive practices - such as using elemental or archetypal pairings instead of gendered roles in ritual, crafting altars that honor the spectrum of identity, or inviting self-blessing rites to celebrate each witch's unique essence. At the same time, many of these covens acknowledge that witchcraft has its roots in fertility-based traditions, where the sacred union of masculine and feminine energies represented the life-giving cycles of nature. Rather than dismiss this foundation, they revere it - honoring procreative energy as a universal force that transcends gender identity. In this way, they hold space for the symbolic great rite, even if they choose not to embody its binary roles. This approach allows for deep authenticity - a reminder that witchcraft evolves not by erasing its roots, but by nourishing new growth from them. At its core, witchcraft celebrates life, love, and the joy of honing your craft with people you trust. Whether it's the pleasure of being a witch or the profound satisfaction of working magick with kindred spirits, all acts of love and pleasure are sacred to the Goddess.

DECIDING ON COVEN ETHICS AND RESPONSIBILITIES

Establishing clear ethics and responsibilities is crucial for the success and harmony of your coven. These guidelines should be written up in the coven's Book of Shadows before the first gathering. Here is a suggested list:

1. Honor personal commitments: Once you have committed to being in your coven, stand by that commitment for the agreed time (usually a year and a day). Respect the personal commitment each member has made with their effort and time by being consistent in your attitude and the application of your own efforts.
2. Keep the coven sacred: Do not bring personal dramas to gatherings. A coven meets "between the worlds" and should serve as an oasis from the trials and tribulations of everyday life.
3. Commit to creating a strong group mind: Engage in coven dedications and meditations daily, and practice personal lifestyle choices that support the goals of the coven.

It's helpful to have signed statements of intent in your coven's Book of Shadows, where every new member copies the agreed list of ethics and responsibilities and signs to confirm their respect and acknowledgment of the depth of their commitment.

> In my last 20 years of the craft, I have experienced increasingly profound communications with ancient goddesses and gods, particularly Sekhmet. They choose to speak to me; I don't ask for anything from them. I simply venerate, worship, and do what they ask of me. I am convinced we have been created so that these amorphous energies can know themselves through our form and thought, just as they would know themselves through butterflies and spiders, galaxies and grubs - all of creation. Nowhere have I experienced this more profoundly than in my new home of Egypt.
>
> So trust what comes through and speaks uniquely to you . . . and your coven.

CHOOSING YOUR PATRON GOD/DESS

Selecting a patron god or goddess for your coven can be an inspiring and empowering experience. While it's not essential, many covens choose a deity whose attributes reflect the personality and values of the group. My first coven, the Dark Light of Lilith Coven, chose Lilith as our patron goddess. Lilith, often regarded as the first feminist, was a perfect symbol for our strong, all-female group.

In myth, Lilith is a figure of defiance, independence, and empowerment. Cast out of Eden for refusing to submit to Adam, she embodies the power of saying no to subjugation and yes to autonomy. Lilith's energy is rebellious, unapologetic, and deeply aligned with the principles of self-respect, equality, and sovereignty - qualities we celebrated in our coven. Her presence guided us as we embraced our own power, supported each other's growth, and explored the mysteries of the craft together.

Creating your own god/dess

If none of the deities from the world's many pantheons resonate with your coven, you can create a deity that reflects your unique values and purpose. Here's how:

1. **List qualities:** Define the traits you want your deity to embody. Is it a deity of courage, love, wisdom, or transformation? Consider archetypes like maiden, mother, or crone; youth, warrior, or sage. Perhaps it takes the form of an animal, a hybrid, or something otherworldly.
2. **Develop a myth:** Create a story that describes your deity's origins and purpose. What is its realm, and how does it manifest? Use visual inspiration to bring its world to life.
3. **Name your deity:** Choose a name that resonates with the essence of your deity.
4. **Meditate and conjure:** Gather as a group to meditate on your deity, channeling collective energy and intention toward bringing it into being.
5. **Offer regular devotions:** Make offerings that align with your deity's attributes. For instance, a sea goddess might be honored with seashells or salt water. The more energy you invest, the more your deity will manifest as a unique spiritual presence for your coven.

Exploring the divine

Some may find the idea of creating a god or goddess unconventional, even sacrilegious. Yet, all deities can be seen as archetypes - manifestations of human consciousness, reflecting the qualities and ideals of the societies that venerate them. For example, modern icons like Maya Angelou, with her powerful words and unwavering advocacy for equality and resilience; Nelson Mandela, a beacon of strength, forgiveness, and unyielding determination for justice; David Attenborough, whose work inspires a deep respect for the interconnectedness of all life; and Frida Kahlo, an artist whose courage, creativity, and unapologetic authenticity transformed pain into beauty and empowerment - all can be viewed as contemporary archetypes. These figures remind us of the transformative power of humanity, resilience, and creativity.

However, this perspective is just one lens. You may prefer to work with ancient deities who have been worshipped for millennia. These timeless energies hold power not only in their historical significance but also in the collective consciousness of those who continue to honor them.

In my personal journey, I've had profound encounters with ancient goddesses and gods, particularly Sekhmet, the lion-headed goddess of healing, war, and transformation. Living in Egypt has deepened my relationship with these divine energies. They choose when and how to communicate, and I honor them not by asking for favors but by listening and acting in alignment with their guidance.

Whether you connect with Lilith, Sekhmet, or a deity you and your coven create together, remember that your relationship with the divine is personal and ever-evolving. Some believe that gods and goddesses are manifestations of our collective unconscious, while others see them as eternal beings who transcend time and space. Both perspectives are valid.

Trust your path

Choosing your patron deity is a journey of discovery - one that speaks uniquely to you and your coven. Lilith taught me the power of independence, the strength of community, and the importance of embracing the shadows as part of the light. Nelson Mandela inspires us to seek justice, forgiveness, and strength in unity. David Attenborough reminds us to honor the sacredness of the earth, and Frida Kahlo shows us how to transform pain into power and authenticity into art.

Wherever your path leads, trust what resonates with your spirit and the energy of your group so that your choice of a patron god or goddess empowers your coven and illuminates your individual and collective magickal journey.

NAMING YOUR COVEN

Naming your coven is a sacred act, a magickal christening that sets the tone and intention for your gatherings. You might find inspiration in your patron god or goddess, as we did with our Dark Light of Lilith coven, where Lilith's fierce independence and wisdom guided our rituals and practices.

Alternatively, you could draw upon the natural world for inspiration. Flowers and fruits carry potent symbolism and vibrant energies. I remember the first coven gathering I ever attended, hosted by the Eldergrove Coven, named after the sacred elder tree, revered by the Celts for its protective and healing qualities. Such names ground your group in ancient wisdom and natural power.

Crystals and mythical creatures also make enchanting names. Imagine the mystique of the Coven of the Amethyst Phoenix, where transformation and spiritual clarity reign supreme. Or perhaps the allure of the Sapphire Serpent Coven, embodying wisdom and intuition. While a name like the Coven of the Emerald Dragon might conjure images of martial arts legends, it could equally evoke a sense of fierce, protective energy.

The key is to be inventive. Choose a name that excites and inspires you, one that encapsulates the essence of your coven. This name will be a banner under which you gather, a symbol of your collective spirit and the magickal tapestry you are weaving together.

CHOOSING YOUR PERSONAL MAGICKAL NAME

Choosing your personal magickal name is a deeply personal and transformative act, often marking a significant milestone in your spiritual journey. In traditional covens, magickal names are traditionally bestowed upon members during initiation.

A magickal name can serve as a powerful symbol of your spiritual identity, reflecting your intent and aspirations within the craft and thus becoming a beacon of your inner power. Every name holds inherent magick, whether you decide to keep your given name (with a new appreciation of its inherent power) or adopt a new one. Consider the numerology associated with your chosen name to ensure it aligns positively with your magickal goals. Reflect on the symbolism and meaning behind potential names: your magickal name should resonate deeply with you - the one that gives you goosebumps and just feels "right."

Once you have chosen a name, you may wish to perform a naming ritual to formally adopt it and reinforce its power and significance in your practices.

Personal naming ceremony

To perform a personal naming ceremony, find a quiet, sacred space where you feel connected to your inner self. Light a white candle and some incense and place a small bowl of water and a dish of salt before you. Close your eyes, take a few deep breaths, and center yourself. Sprinkle a pinch of salt into the water, stir it with your finger, and then flick the salted water in a circle around you, saying, "*I cleanse and consecrate this space.*" Hold your chosen magickal name in your mind and speak it aloud, saying, "*I am [Magickal Name], and I walk my path with clarity and purpose.*" Dip your fingers again in the water and anoint your forehead, heart, and hands, saying, "*By earth, air, fire, and water, I bless and welcome my magickal name.*" Take a moment to feel the power of your new name resonating within you, then extinguish the candle with a single breath, clearing your path to move forward in your life, carrying your new identity with confidence and grace to your coven's ceremony.

NAMING CEREMONY TO WELCOME A NEW COVEN MEMBER

Preparation

- ★ Gather in a circle with the new member at the center.
- ★ Place a small altar in the middle with a white candle, a bowl of water, a dish of salt, and incense.

Opening

- ★ Begin by lighting the white candle on the altar.
- ★ The facilitator or leader says: "We gather here, united with the divine, to welcome our new sister/brother/sibling into this sacred circle of magick and connection."

Cleansing

- ★ Each coven member takes a turn sprinkling a few grains of salt into the bowl of water, saying: *"We purify this space and welcome [New Member's Name] into our circle with open hearts."*

Invocation

- ★ Light the incense and pass it around the circle. Each member breathes in the scent, visualizing the new member strengthening the bond of the coven.
- ★ The facilitator or leader invokes the elements, saying: "Earth, air, fire, and water, we honor your presence and blessings for this sacred naming ceremony."

Naming

- ★ The new member steps forward and announces their chosen magickal name, saying: *"I am [Magickal Name]. I embrace my path and my place within this coven."*
- ★ The facilitator or leader anoints the new member's forehead with the blessed water, saying: "Welcome, [Magickal Name], to our circle of trust, love, and magick. May your path be illuminated, and may you grow with us in harmony."

Blessing

- ★ Each coven member places a hand on the new member's shoulder, forming a chain of connection, and says in unison: *"Aligned with the divine, we bless you, [Magickal Name], and welcome you as our sister/brother/sibling in magick."*

Closing

- ★ The facilitator or leader concludes the ceremony, saying: "Our magick grows stronger with your presence. Welcome to the circle. May our bond remain unbroken and carried within our hearts. Always merry meet. Always merry part."
- ★ Extinguish the candle, signaling the end of the ceremony.

Celebration

- ★ Share food, drinks, and joyful conversation to celebrate the new member's arrival into the coven. Let the gathering be a time of connection and warmth, honoring and charging the shared journey ahead.

DECIDING WHERE TO GATHER TOGETHER

Finding a safe and welcoming space for your coven gatherings can be a delicate task. While many dedicated Wiccan, pagan, and spiritual sanctuaries have been established - beautiful parklands and retreats where witches and pagans can gather freely and perform

their rituals without fear of harassment - these may not be accessible for you, so instead consider these potential gathering spots:

- ★ Private backyards: Intimate and secure, offering privacy and a connection to nature.
- ★ Large living rooms or private balconies: Cozy and convenient for smaller gatherings.
- ★ Community halls: Available for rent and often come with the benefit of indoor facilities.
- ★ Pagan-friendly retreats and campgrounds: In Australia and the US, there are many options available across the states, with numerous non-discriminatory campgrounds and retreat spaces that welcome spiritual and nature-based gatherings. When choosing a site, look for features like privacy from the public, open space for ritual circles, fire pits or designated flame areas, and a general openness to alternative or earth-based spiritual practices.

Places to avoid:

- ★ Public parks during the day: Unless you have explicit permission from the local council, these areas can attract unwanted attention and disturbance
- ★ Parks and beaches at night: This can be dangerous, as you never know who might show up. Even the most potent circle of pure protection might not keep away potential troublemakers.
- ★ Vacant properties: Trespassing is illegal and could result in arrest.

Be creative in finding your safe space. Remember to scout your chosen location during the day if you plan to meet at night. Familiarize yourself with the terrain to avoid any mishaps - like sliding off a roof and into a swimming pool!

CHAPTER 6

SPARK TO CIRCLE: FORGING YOUR COVEN

After completing the first essential steps - gathering interested and committed potential coven members and securing a location for our magickal gatherings - it is important to agree on some basic tools of witchcraft that each member would have. It is never necessary to spend a fortune on elaborate props: a few well-selected or self-crafted tools are more than enough to assist in practicing the craft.

Before officially dedicating your coven, hold an initial meeting to which everyone can bring their personal tools. This is to agree on the basic tools each member should have, so no one feels overwhelmed or out of place.

Finances may be a consideration, especially when young and still finding your way. The value of an athame doesn't come from its price but from the intent and energy brought to it. A simple pointed finger could channel just as much power as the fanciest blade!

TOOLS

Here are the basic items that my first coven agreed were essential for practicing the rituals and spells we worked on together:

Personal altar

- ★ Athame: For casting circles and channeling energy (representing male energy and the element of fire).
- ★ Pentacle: I used a large flat mother-of-pearl shell with five embedded pearls in it, aligning with the pentagram's five points, to represent earth.
- ★ Chalice: For libations and toasting, symbolizing female energy.
- ★ Incense: Representing the element of air.
- ★ Bowl: For the element of water, often filled with seashells when not in use.
- ★ Candles: Representing fire.
- ★ Book of Shadows: For personal record-keeping.

Extras

- ★ Small cauldron: Perfect for burning petitions.
- ★ Wand: For conjuring and directing energy, distinct from the athame.
- ★ Mortar and pestle: For blending incenses and powders.

In addition to personal altars, each of us created a coven shrine. This shared space reflected the spirit of our group and honored Lilith, our patron goddess. We chose basic items for the shrine and added personal touches over time, making it a reflection of our unity and creativity.

Coven stash

We also agreed on a coven stash of tools and magickal goods. Since we didn't have a permanent location, these items were usually kept by me and circulated as needed. Some of the items included:

- ★ Coven Book of Shadows
- ★ Statue of Lilith
- ★ Coven candle: Only lit at gatherings.
- ★ Coven totem: A dried wolf's heart, lovingly referred to as the "heart de lobos" by Lupita, symbolized our coven's strength and unity.
- ★ Incense thurible or burner: Essential for purifying spaces and creating atmosphere.
- ★ Altar cloth: To transform any surface into a sacred space.
- ★ A supply of candles and incense
- ★ Books for research and inspiration

CREATIVE BEGINNINGS

Our meetings weren't always in grand settings. One of our first gatherings was on the roof of my friend's house! We learned quickly that preparation and safety were just as important as magick. For midnight gatherings, we always scoped out locations during the day to avoid surprises - like accidentally walking too close to a cliff's edge!

By being resourceful and creative, we found ways to make our gatherings meaningful.

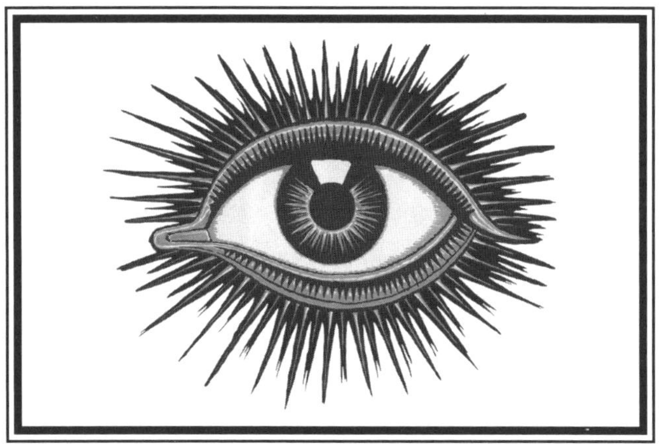

PRACTICAL AND MAGICKAL

Looking back, my first coven taught me that witchcraft thrives on balance - practicality paired with magick. Whether you're using a thrifted chalice or your favorite pen as a wand, the true power comes from your intent. The lessons I learned with Tri and Lupita remain with me, a reminder of how magick is created not by the tools themselves but by the energy and spirit we bring to them.

THE COVEN LIBRARY

It's so wonderful to see the book witch thriving in this digital age.

Between you and your coven members, there may be a significant number of books, and you might think it appropriate to combine your collections to form a coven library. Alternatively, you could chip in funds to purchase books specifically for a shared library. If you do this, make sure to keep track of them by recording each book's name, the lending date, and the name of the borrower.

An expansive idea is to stick a book plate inside the front cover so that everyone who reads and interacts with the book can write their name and comment on how helpful they found it. This not only helps in tracking but also creates a shared history and sense of community around your collective knowledge.

SHOPPING FOR COVEN SUPPLIES

Shopping for coven supplies is an exciting part of the journey! Do some research and make a few calls to ensure you can find the various (and sometimes obscure) items you may need. Doing this as a group is a fantastic way to bond and for everyone to gain a good understanding of the uses of different items. If you live in an area without esoteric or New Age supply stores, you can forage or order things online. But at the same time be mindful of the carbon footprint you leave, the radiation every item is blasted with, and the accumulation of energy. Clear and purify everything by smudging with white sage, frankincense, or sandalwood smoke . . . or leaving out in the full moonlight.

You may find it rewarding to make some of your personal and coven tools yourselves. This could involve attending a workshop together or simply sitting down and getting creative as a group.

The more grassroots interaction you have, the stronger your coven bond will be, making your activities together more effective and rewarding.

CAN SOMEONE ELSE TOUCH MY ATHAME?

It's generally considered good magickal manners not to just pick up someone else's personal magickal stash. Through repeated use, certain objects like athames and wands can absorb the energy of their "owner" and become specifically aligned to them. In theory, someone else picking them up without respecting the significance of this magickal bond could interfere with it and the object's effectiveness in completing its magickal task. So always ask the owner if it's okay to pick something up, even if you just need to move it to make room on the altar for the cauldron or another tool.

However, shared coven tools are different. It can be really beneficial for everyone to handle them, as they will be imbued with the collective energy of the entire coven, enhancing their power and connection.

SETTING UP YOUR PERSONAL ALTAR

Here's what you need to create your altar.

- A candle for fire:
    - Northern hemisphere: Place this in the southern quarter, symbolizing the life-giving fire of the sun.
    - Southern hemisphere: Place this in the northern quarter, aligning with the sun's path.

- A crystal for earth:
    - Northern hemisphere: Place this in the northern quarter, connecting to the grounding energy of the earth.
    - Southern hemisphere: Place this in the southern quarter, reflecting the land's steady presence.

- Your pentacle with your athame on it: Usually placed in the center for balance and focus.
- Incense for air: Place this in the eastern quarter, as it represents dawn, intellect, and inspiration.
- A bowl of water: Place this in the western quarter, symbolizing emotions, intuition, and the flow of life.
- Chalice: a vessel for libations and toasting, representing the divine feminine and receptivity.
- An image of the Goddess and God (optional): These can be physical representations, statues, or artwork that resonate with you.
- An altar cloth (optional): You may choose a cloth to reflect the seasons, your personal aesthetic, or your magickal intent. However, some prefer to leave the altar bare to connect directly with its surface.

PERSONAL COVEN SHRINES

In addition to your personal solitary altar, it's beneficial to create a personal coven shrine if you're part of a group. This shrine features objects specifically tied to your coven and its patron God or Goddess. You may also include photos or representations of your fellow coveners, fostering a sense of connection even when you're apart.

If you're just beginning, starting with a coven shrine is a great idea. Over time, as your experience deepens and your personal practices grow, you can build a personal altar as well.

Empowering your shrine

Your coven shrine isn't just symbolic - it's an active portal to your covenworld. Begin each day by meditating and performing a morning dedication at your shrine. Over time, the energy you channel and project during these practices will imbue the objects on your shrine with power, creating a potent feedback loop and a tangible link to the shared intentions and magick of your coven.

THE COVEN BOOK OF SHADOWS

A Book of Shadows is a sacred record of magickal workings, rituals, and methods. Each witch can have a personal Book of Shadows, and there is also a coven Book of Shadows, which serves as a communal repository of shared knowledge and experiences.

Purpose and importance

The coven Book of Shadows is a collaborative collection of the group's rituals, spells, and magickal experiences. It is a living document that grows and evolves with the coven, reflecting the collective journey and wisdom of its members. Each entry is a testament to the coven's shared magickal journey and spiritual growth.

Structure and maintenance

Maintaining the coven Book of Shadows is a shared responsibility. When a member writes a ritual, they add it to the coven Book and share copies with other members, who then include it in their personal Books of Shadows, adding their own notes and insights. This practice ensures that everyone has a comprehensive record of the coven's magickal practices and personal reflections.

Inspiration for your Book of Shadows

The physical form of your Book of Shadows can be as unique and creative as the magick it contains. Here are some inspirational ideas for crafting your Book:

- ★ Recycled paper: Opt for eco-friendly recycled paper, which adds a rustic and earthy touch and is energetically aligned with earth love and conservation values.
- ★ Engraved wood cover: a wooden cover with engravings will confer empowerment and can be charged energetically with sigils and symbols.
- ★ Faux leather binding: Faux leather can provide a classic, durable binding that evokes ancient wisdom.
- ★ Cord wrap: Wrapping your Book in a cord not only secures it but also can be tied off in magickal knots to keep the information contained within charged and potent.
- ★ Personalized decorations: Embellish your Book with symbols, crystals, or dried herbs that resonate with your practice.

Personalization and ritual

To deeply personalize and consecrate your Book of Shadows, consider a dedication ritual. Some covens mark their Book with a drop of their blood, symbolizing a powerful bond with the magickal content within. (For a full description of this process, see the "Dedicate your coven" chapter.)

Using the Book of Shadows

Regularly update your Book of Shadows with new rituals, spells, and experiences. Reflect on your entries, noting any outcomes or insights gained from your magickal workings. This practice not only keeps your Book current but also helps you learn and grow from your experiences.

By thoughtfully creating and maintaining your coven Book of Shadows, you cultivate a powerful tool that reflects your collective magickal journey, serving as both a record and a source of inspiration for your continued practice.

COVEN CLOTHING

Witchcraft is not a fashion statement, so no pointy hats and dark cloaks are required at coven gatherings. However, if you wish to wear these traditional accoutrements, feel free. Practicality and safety should guide your choices. As advised by Hawthorn, the High Priestess of Eldergrove Coven, "Don't wear your cloaks into circle - they fall and drape all over the place, knocking over candles, sweeping items off the altar, and are generally very hazardous!"

Simple clothing in circle is usually best. Basic black robes with slim long sleeves can offer both a unified and practical look.

General guidelines for coven clothing

- ★ Simplicity and safety: Choose simple, comfortable clothing that allows free movement and avoids hazards like tripping or knocking over items.
- ★ Respect for financial circumstances: Avoid requiring expensive clothing to ensure inclusivity. Simple attire in black is often sufficient,

with variations for specific Sabbats (e.g., white for Imbolc, red for Beltane, green for Yule, orange for Lammas). Or Sabbats can be celebrated with colored and themed accessories rather than different colored robes.

★ Witchy jewelry: Adorn yourself with meaningful jewelry, such as pentacles, gemstone necklaces, or cultural beads. These items can enhance your connection to the craft and to each other.
★ Bare feet: Many witches prefer to go barefoot to feel more connected to the earth during rituals.
★ Personal grooming: Consider taking a shower before gatherings to cleanse the accumulated energy of the day and approach the ritual with a fresh, clear mind.

Traditional and group jewelry

In traditional groups like Gardnerian and Alexandrian covens, it is customary for women to wear a large silver bangle or ring and for men to wear a brass or copper bangle or ring to signify their membership. As a group, it can be meaningful to agree on a piece of jewelry that each member wears, similar to a wedding ring. These pieces can be consecrated and ceremonially put on during the coven dedication ceremony. Options include matching pentacle necklaces, onyx rings, or carved silver bracelets.

By thoughtfully considering your coven attire, you can create a cohesive, respectful, and energetically powerful gathering space.

Being skyclad at coven gatherings

Being skyclad, or practicing ritual in the nude, is a tradition in some witchcraft practices, but it is by no means mandatory. It's entirely up to each individual and coven to decide what feels right for them.

The purpose of being skyclad is multifaceted. It aims to liberate us from our preconceived notions of class, culture, and societal norms. By shedding our clothes, we symbolically shed our external identities and social statuses, allowing us to connect more deeply with our true selves and with each other. Being skyclad is also a celebration of the extraordinary human form in all its diverse expressions, honoring the body as a vessel of life and a conduit for spiritual energy. The only time I participated in a skyclad gathering was early in my craft and it is seared in my memory as one of the most joyful and free experiences of my life.

Personal comfort and self-love

If being skyclad makes you feel uncomfortable, it's important to honor those feelings. You should never feel pressured to do anything that doesn't resonate with you. It's as simple as that. However, it can also be an opportunity for self-reflection. Consider examining why you feel uncomfortable. If it stems from not being proud of your body or feeling uncomfortable in your own skin, you might benefit from self-love rituals to affirm and appreciate your unique physical beauty.

SELF-LOVE RITUALS

Engaging in suggested self-love rituals can help you build a positive relationship with your body. Mirror work: Spend time looking at yourself in the mirror, focusing on what you love about your body. Speak affirmations aloud, such as, "I love and accept myself completely."

- ★ Sacred bathing: Take a ritual bath with essential oils, herbs, and candles. As you soak, visualize cleansing away negative thoughts about your body and infusing yourself with self-love and acceptance.
- ★ Body blessing: Touch and bless each part of your body, expressing gratitude for all it does for you. You can use a favorite oil or enchanted lotion during this ritual.
- ★ Journaling: Write about your feelings toward your body and explore the roots of any negative self-image. Follow up with affirmations and positive statements about your body.

ENCHANTED BODY-BLESSING LOTION (GENDER-NEUTRAL)

INGREDIENTS:

- 2 tbsp unscented natural lotion or body butter (shea or cocoa base work beautifully)
- 2 drops frankincense essential oil - for spiritual communion
- 2 drops rose essential oil - for self-love, heart opening, and compassion
- 1 drop sandalwood essential oil - for grounding and sacred presence
- OPTIONAL: a pinch of mica shimmer powder - to invite radiant light
- OPTIONAL: a few drops of moon water or floral water - for energetic activation

Mantra to whisper or speak as you apply it:

Thank you body, born of stars
Whole and holy, as you are.

Apply mindfully to your body during your self-blessing rite. It can also be used during moon rituals, after ritual baths, or whenever reconnection to your sacred self is needed.

MANAGING COVEN FINANCES

Managing finances as a coven can be a straightforward and rewarding process that ensures financial equality, supports group activities, and enhances the quality of shared experiences. Below are some proactive and simple strategies for handling coven finances.

Sharing expenses

For smaller covens, it's easy to chip in and share expenses. Members can take turns buying necessary items. For example, one person might buy candles while another brings juice and snacks for after the ritual. This approach promotes fairness and shared responsibility.

Potluck gatherings

For larger gatherings or special events, consider organizing potluck affairs where everyone brings a plate of food and a bottle of drink. Each person can also contribute items needed for the ritual, such as candles or flowers. This not only spreads the cost but also encourages participation and community spirit.

Coven kitty

For larger covens, establishing a coven kitty can be very effective. Each member contributes a small amount, such as $10, at each meeting. This pooled fund can be used to buy supplies, books, and other necessities. This ensures that the financial burden is shared equally and the coven can collectively invest in its practices.

Saving for special events

Consider setting up a savings account where members contribute a fixed amount, like $50 each month. This fund can be used for special projects or to finance a shared trip to a sacred site at the end of the year. This way, the coven can plan exciting group activities without putting financial strain on individual members.

Fundraising ideas

There are various ways to raise money for coven activities and expenses:

- ★ GARAGE SALES: Sell items you no longer need (smudge them first and release any energetic ties!).
- ★ CRAFT SALES: Create and sell magickal soaps, incense blends, and other handmade items at pagan festivals and gatherings.
- ★ PERFORMANCES: If members are musically inclined, consider putting on shows and donating the proceeds to the coven kitty.

Contributions and energy exchange

In modern times, it's important to recognize the value of magickal wisdom and the time, energy, and resources that go into sharing it. While the craft has traditionally emphasized the spirit of generosity, it is perfectly reasonable to charge a fair fee for workshops, teaching, or magickal help, especially when these offerings require significant preparation, travel, or accommodation.

Charging for your time and expertise isn't about profiting from spirituality - it's about creating an "energy exchange" that honors the work and ensures sustainability. A modest fee can help offset costs and reflect the value of the knowledge being shared. Consider offering a sliding scale, or you could invite participants to make a financial or time donation to a charitable cause as part of the magickal circle of giving.

Ultimately, the balance lies in valuing your work while staying true to the principles of the craft: respect, reciprocity, and community.

Balancing financial and spiritual goals

It's important to ensure that money does not come between you and your craft. Financial contributions should be voluntary and managed in a way that supports the coven's goals without causing stress or inequality. Appointing someone to keep track of expenses can help maintain transparency and fairness.

TRAVEL AND RETREATS

Consider planning trips to significant spiritual locations. These excursions can be enriching and enhance the bond between coven members. Here are some destinations with special appeal for magickal people:

- ★ AMERICA: New Orleans with its Voodoo museums and mysterious swamplands, Salem in Massachusetts with its rich witchcraft history, Taos in New Mexico with its vibrant spiritual community, Joshua Tree in California known for its unique desert landscape, and magickal Topanga Canyon in Malibu, reminiscent of the 1970s spiritual vibe.
- ★ AUSTRALIA: Hanging Rock in Victoria, Byron Bay in New South Wales, Arnhem Land in the Northern Territory, and Cradle Mountain in Tasmania are extraordinary locations rich in natural energy. These places offer profound connections to the ancient wisdom and sacred traditions of Aboriginal culture, inviting deep reflection and spiritual alignment.
- ★ BALI: Known for its vibrant spiritual culture, lush landscapes, and temples, Bali offers a serene and inspirational environment for magickal practices.
- ★ CAMBODIA: Walk among the 12th-century towers of Angkor Wat, where stone and jungle entwine. The craftsmanship, scale, and astrological alignment make it one of the great sacred wonders of the world.
- ★ EGYPT: Visit the pyramids and contemplate their mysteries. Enter ancient temples to connect with the deep spiritual and historical roots of early magick and ritual.

- ★ **Ireland:** The Emerald Isle, with its fairy folklore, ancient monuments, and lush landscapes, offers a deep connection to Celtic traditions and magickal practices.
- ★ **Scotland:** With its mystical highlands, stone circles, and rich Celtic heritage, Scotland is a magickal destination full of history and natural beauty.

By thoughtfully managing finances and planning enriching activities, your coven can foster financial equality, strengthen community bonds, and create memorable, high-quality shared experiences.

And please, if you would like a planned coven magickal experience hosted by me, let me know. Since 2024 I have been offering nourishing spiritual adventures in Egypt and Bali . . . and beyond! Visit my website fionahorne.com for more information.

INCORPORATING AS A SPIRITUAL ORGANIZATION

Incorporating your coven as a spiritual organization can offer significant advantages, especially if you have plans to expand and build a community of service and spiritual support:

Benefits of incorporating as a spiritual organization

1. Tax exemptions: Spiritual organizations often qualify for various tax exemptions, including property tax, income tax, and sales tax. This can free up more resources for your coven's activities and community services.
2. Legal recognition: Incorporation provides legal recognition and protection for your coven. This can help in securing locations for gatherings and events.
3. Grants and donations: Incorporated spiritual organizations are eligible to receive grants and donations, which can be used to support and expand your community services.
4. Formal structure: Incorporating establishes a formal structure, which can help in the organization and management of your coven. This includes creating bylaws, appointing officers, and setting clear roles and responsibilities.
5. Community building: As a recognized spiritual organization, your coven can more easily build and grow a community, offering spiritual support, educational programs, and charitable services.

Steps to incorporate as a spiritual organization

1. Consult an expert: Seek advice from a legal or financial professional specializing in non-profits or religious institutions in your country. They can provide tailored guidance based on your local laws and requirements.
2. Draft governing documents: Prepare bylaws or a constitution that outlines the purpose, structure, and governance of your organization. This document is critical for incorporation and establishing credibility.
3. Choose a name: Select a unique and meaningful name that reflects your group's identity, mission, and spiritual focus. Be sure to check that the name is not already in use in your region.
4. Register with authorities: File the necessary incorporation documents with the appropriate government agency in your country. This may include articles of incorporation, a constitution, or other foundational paperwork, often accompanied by a registration fee.
5. Obtain a tax identification number: Apply for a tax identification number or equivalent in your country. In the US, this is an EIN from the IRS; in other countries, consult your local tax authority for the appropriate registration process.
6. Apply for tax-exempt status (if applicable): Many countries allow religious organizations to apply for tax-exempt status. In the US, this involves submitting IRS Form 1023. In other regions, you may need to work with local tax offices or regulatory bodies. This step can be complex, so expert assistance is highly recommended.
7. Form a governing body: Establish a board of directors or trustees to oversee the operations, finances, and governance of the organization. This body ensures that the organization adheres to its governing documents and mission.

8. Develop a mission statement: Craft a clear and inspiring mission statement that defines your organization's purpose and goals. This statement helps attract members, supporters, and potential donors while providing direction for activities.
9. Implement record-keeping systems: Set up systems for maintaining accurate records of meetings, finances, membership, and other essential activities. Transparent and organized record-keeping is crucial for legal compliance and building trust within your community.
10. Understand local laws and cultural sensitivities: Be mindful of the cultural and legal landscape in your region. Ensure your organization respects local customs and operates within the boundaries of applicable laws to maintain credibility and harmony within your community.

BUILDING A COMMUNITY OF SERVICE AND SPIRITUAL SUPPORT

Incorporating as a spiritual organization provides a strong foundation for growing your coven into a vibrant community. With the legal and financial benefits in place, you can focus on expanding your services and outreach. Consider offering:

- Educational programs: Provide classes and workshops on various aspects of witchcraft, spirituality, and personal development.
- Community services: Organize volunteer activities, support local charities, and offer spiritual counselling and support to those in need.
- Ritual and worship: Hold regular rituals, Sabbats, and Esbats, creating a sacred space for members to connect and practice their faith.
- Support groups: Create support groups for members to share experiences, provide mutual support, and build strong connections within the community.

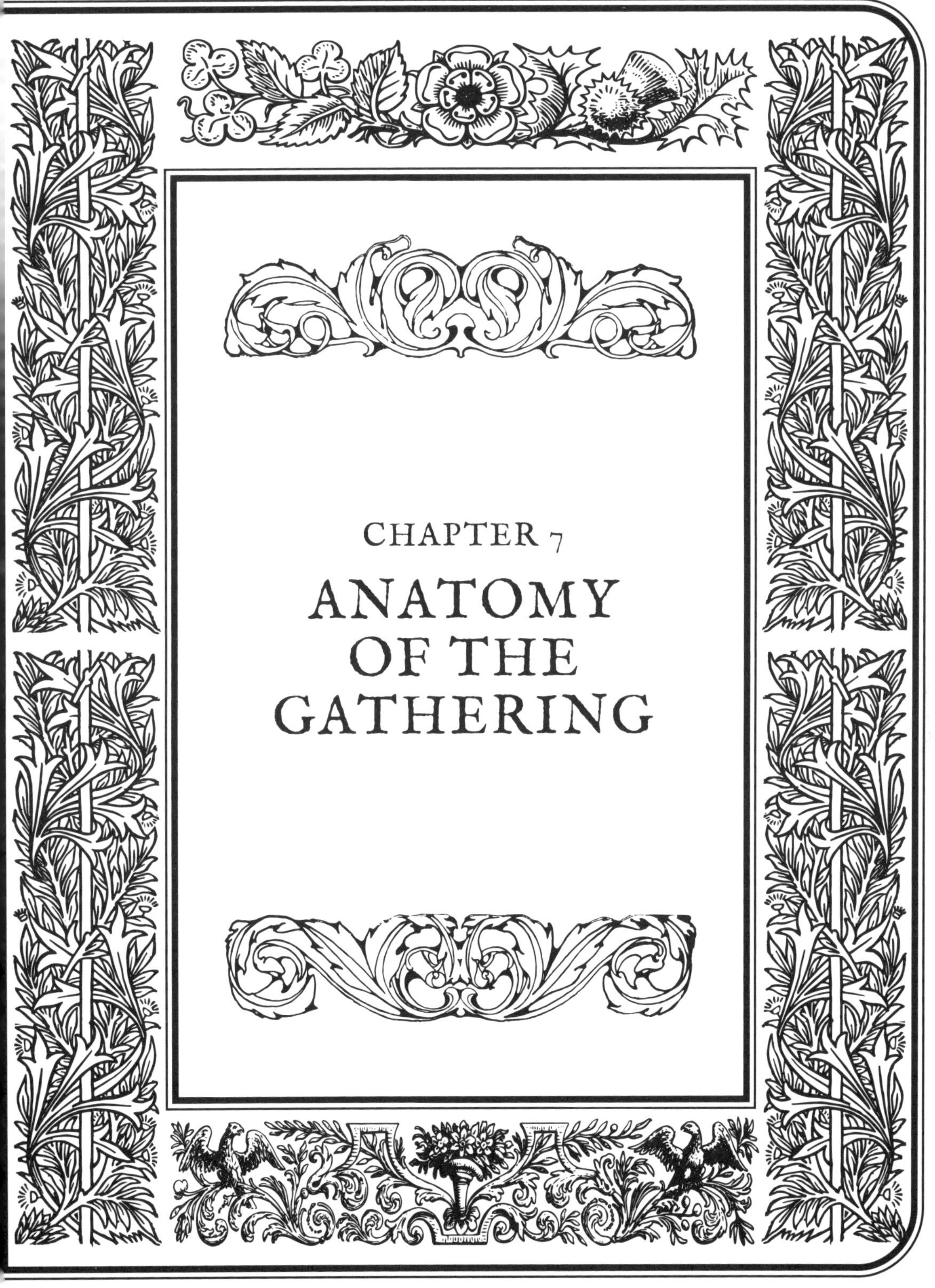

CHAPTER 7

ANATOMY OF THE GATHERING

Your first coven meeting doesn't need to be a nerve-wracking experience. With proper planning and a sense of adventure (and humor!), you can have a marvelous, intense experience that gets your coven off to a great start.

PREPARING FOR YOUR MEETING

Writing your rituals

One way to ensure a powerful and transformative gathering is to write your own circle-casting ritual, elemental and God/dess invocations, and raising power chants. This personalized touch helps everyone connect deeply with the words and the intent behind the ritual.

Focus and intent

It's important to focus on the task at hand when entering the ritual space. Leave personal discussions for later during the grounding and feasting. When you step into the sacred space, leave the everyday world behind and immerse yourself in the magickal work.

Handling nerves

Feeling nervous is completely natural, especially when leading a ritual for the first time. Embrace the nerves - they're a sign that you care deeply about creating a meaningful experience. Here are some techniques to help you manage them and find your flow:

- **Ground yourself:** Before the ritual, take a moment to stand barefoot on the ground if possible. Imagine roots extending from your feet into the earth, anchoring you and drawing strength from its steady, grounding energy.
- **Breathe mindfully:** Use a simple breathing technique to calm your mind. Inhale deeply for a count of four, hold for four, exhale for four, and pause for four. Repeat this cycle a few times to reset your energy and focus.
- **Visualize success:** Close your eyes and visualize yourself leading the ritual with ease and grace. Imagine the energy flowing naturally, the group responding positively, and the magick taking shape. Visualization can boost confidence and set the tone for the ritual.
- **Prepare a grounding object:** Keep a small object, like a crystal or a charm, in your pocket or on the altar. If you feel overwhelmed, touch it as a reminder of your strength and connection to the moment.
- **Rely on a script or notes:** It's okay to have a written outline of the ritual or a few key points jotted down. Knowing you have a guide to refer to can ease pressure and help you stay on track.
- **Lean on your coven:** Remember, you're not alone. Your coven is there to support you, and they'll appreciate your effort and intention. Trust in the collective energy of the group to guide and uplift you.
- **Acknowledge the nerves:** If you feel the tension building, mentally acknowledge it. Say to yourself, *"I feel nervous, and that's okay."* This simple act of self-compassion can reduce the intensity of those feelings.
- **Focus on service:** Shift your focus from yourself to the purpose of the ritual and the energy you're raising for the group. When your attention is on serving the greater good, nerves tend to take a back seat.

Remember, leading a ritual is not about perfection - it's about presence. Trust in your preparation, your connection to the Divine, and your ability to create a space where magick can flourish. With time and experience, confidence will come naturally.

CASTING THE CIRCLE

Casting a circle creates a sacred space that contains desired energies and keeps out unwanted ones. Imagine the circle as a sphere surrounding you, above and below. The strength of this circle depends on how vividly you and your coveners can visualize it into being.

Basic steps for casting the circle

1. Choose your tool: Stand and point in front of you your athame, wand, index finger, feather, or chosen tool.
2. Visualize light: See light streaming from the tool's point.
3. Trace the circle: Move in a sunwise direction (clockwise in the northern hemisphere, counterclockwise in the southern hemisphere), tracing the light in a circle around you.

Practical considerations

- ★ Circle size and shape: While some traditions specify exact measurements for circles, the most important aspect is the intent and focus behind them. You can use the power of numbers, like nine feet for wisdom, but it's not strictly necessary.
- ★ Physical markings: You can mark the circle with tea light candles in glass jars for safety, or trace with salt or use other objects and symbols that resonate with your practice. The physical form of the circle enhances the atmosphere and aids visualization, but remember that the true circle exists in the spiritual realm.

SACRED CIRCLE SIZES AND THEIR MAGICKAL INTENTIONS

- A three-foot (.91-metre) circle represents creation and the sacred trinity. It's ideal for quick solo spells or workings where focused intention is key - perfect for birth energy or new beginnings.
- A five-foot (1.5-metre) circle aligns with elemental balance and harmony. Use this size for connecting with the five elements, casting a pentacle, or performing rituals that seek to restore equilibrium.
- A seven-foot (2-metre) circle is associated with mysticism, spiritual awakening, and protection. It's powerful for inner work, dreamwork, or shielding rituals, especially those involving intuition or higher guidance.
- A nine-foot (2.7-metre) circle represents wisdom and completion. This is a traditional size for coven gatherings, initiations, and deeper spiritual work that calls for collective energy and full-cycle magick.
- An eleven-foot (3.3-metre) circle symbolizes a spiritual doorway or threshold. Use this size for advanced rites, divine insight, and transformation when you're seeking to break through limitations or invite higher frequencies.
- A thirteen-foot (4-metre) circle embodies coven unity and sacred community. It's ideal for full moon rituals, Sabbats, ancestral work, or any gathering that calls upon the full power of the group and the spirit world.

ENCHANTING NUMBERS

Numbers are everywhere, and when you start tuning into them with a witch's eye, they can become secret spells woven through your everyday life. From how many rings you wear on your fingers to how many candles you light to how many drops of essential oil you diffuse, numbers can hold meaning, intention, and magick. Here's a little guide to help you enchant your life, one digit at a time.

0 - Perfect love and perfect trust: Represents the unity of all things, the infinite cycle of life, and the essence of trust in the universe.
1 - The empowered self: Symbolizes individuality, new beginnings, and the strength to stand alone with confidence.
2 - The perfect couple: Denotes partnership, duality, and the harmonious balance of opposites.
3 - Positive and personal power: Encourages self-expression, creativity, and harnessing inner power for positive outcomes.
4 - Balance and harmony: Embodies stability, groundedness, and the ability to create balance in life.
5 - Physical and mental strength: Reflects courage, adaptability, and the endurance to overcome obstacles.
6 - Love and passion: Signifies deep connections, romantic energy, and the power of affection.
7 - Spiritual enlightenment: Highlights inner wisdom, intuition, and the journey toward spiritual growth.
8 - Infinite potential: Emphasizes limitless possibilities, abundance, and the power to achieve greatness.

9 - Wisdom and compassion: Symbolizes profound understanding, empathy, and the compassionate sharing of knowledge.

In our coven's Book of Shadows, we wrote:

The perimeter of the circle is created by the energy channeled by the athame, visualized by the coveners as blue-white light. It can also be physically marked out by salt, a tracing in the earth, or a ring of candles.

INVOCATION OF THE CIRCLE

The wording for invoking the circle is always simple but potent. The person casting the circle stands with their athame, wand, or finger raised while all the coveners focus on visualizing the blue-white light pouring from the tip of the blade, tracing a circle around them. This light then splits into bands above and below, forming a protective sphere. Once the tracing is complete, the circle-caster traces a large pentagram over the circle to seal the process.

Words to recite while tracing the circle

Option one: I conjure thee circle - gate of enlightenment, light around us, light within us.
Option two: I cast this sacred circle, a shield of power and peace, encircling us with love and protection.
Option three: I cast this circle of magick charm. No harm shall enter, no ill shall pass; within, only truth and light shall last.

The tracing of the pentagram can be sealed with a simple powerful statement: *The circle is bound and blessed. So mote it be.*

Typically, one person performs the actions, but everyone can say the words together if desired. Leading the process ensures that the circle is cast with focused intent and unity. Sharing leadership roles within the coven is essential for two reasons: it encourages everyone to be proactive and involved, keeping the workings more potent, and it allows each member to experience both leading and participating in the ritual.

Taking turns as the circle-caster allows each member to deepen their connection to the ritual, whether they are speaking the words and performing the actions or simply visualizing the circle forming.

A note on writing your own invocations

Here's an opportunity to get creative. Personalize your circle invocation to reflect the unique energy and intent of your coven. For example, you might start with:

I conjure thee, circle, so that you may exist between the worlds,
Vibrant and potent, ripe with our dreams and desires.

Or you could use the same words as I use:

I conjure thee circle, the gate of enlightenment.
Above and below. Light around me. Light within me [*or us*].

Remember, the words should inspire and excite you and your coveners, making everyone feel ready for a deeply magickal experience. Personalizing your rituals ensures they resonate powerfully with your group, enhancing the reach and effectiveness of your magick.

I offer a circle casting ritual song on my solo album *Witch Web* available on Spotify, Apple Music, and other streaming services.

THE CIRCLE IS CAST - WHAT'S NEXT?

Once the circle is cast, the next step is to introduce the physical elements of magickal manifestation into the circle: air, earth, fire, and water.

Summoning the elements

Some traditions talk about summoning the guardians of the watchtowers and envisioning metaphysical beings like sylphs (air), undines (water), salamanders (fire), and gnomes (earth) dwelling in the corresponding quarters of your circle. These practices, rooted in Gardnerian magickal traditions and Masonic rituals, are valid and powerful, as they tap into a collective, unconscious projection of these entities.

In an eclectic coven, however, you might choose to reinforce the qualities that the elements represent and visualize them in their natural state. Here's how you can incorporate the elements into your ritual space:

PLACING THE ELEMENTS ON THE ALTAR
From our Book of Shadows:

- ★ EAST/AIR: Incense or a feather if smoke is not allowed
- ★ SOUTH/FIRE: A candle, lit or unlit if flames are not permitted
- ★ WEST/WATER: A bowl of water with a pinch of salt and a seashell
- ★ NORTH/EARTH: A crystal

Note: These are northern hemisphere correspondences. In the southern hemisphere, place fire in the north and earth in the south.

Aligning the elements with the four compass points can harness the earth's electromagnetic poles, enhancing your magickal power. Here's a guide on how to relate to the directions.

ELEMENTAL CORRESPONDENCES

AIR IN THE EAST: The sun rises in the east, symbolizing fresh starts, inspiration, and the winds of change. Air is associated with intellect, communication, and the power of ideas. It brings clarity and movement, encouraging renewal and transformation.

FIRE: Place fire in the south, as this direction aligns with the equator and the sun's warmth and intensity. Fire represents passion, transformation, energy, and the drive to create.

Southern hemisphere: Place fire in the north, reflecting the equator's powerful heat and fiery energy.

WATER IN THE WEST: The west represents the setting sun, endings, and transitions. Water embodies emotions, intuition, and the flow of life's cycles. It is the realm of healing, reflection, and adaptability.

EARTH: Place earth in the north, symbolizing grounding, stability, and the wisdom of the land. The north's cool, steady nature mirrors the strength and endurance of this element.

Southern hemisphere: Place earth in the south, connecting with the solid, nurturing energy of the land below the equator.

INVOCATION OF THE ELEMENTS

As each element is called, the coveners turn to face the corresponding direction and interact with the object representing that element:

- ★ AIR (EAST): Fan the incense with a hand or feather.
- ★ FIRE (SOUTH): Raise the candle to cast its light.
- ★ WATER (WEST): Sprinkle water from your fingertips.
- ★ EARTH (NORTH): Touch the crystal to the ground and then hold it aloft.

INVOCATION EXAMPLE:

I open the quarter of air, to inspire our dreams and lift our spirits.
I open the quarter of fire, to fuel our goals and empower our workings.
I open the quarter of water, to fill our hearts and nourish our potential.
I open the quarter of earth, to anchor our efforts in the physical realm.

Inviting the Goddess and the God

In various traditions, the Goddess and God are respectfully invited into the circle in humble acknowledgment of their wisdom and divine presence. We extend an invitation, trusting that their presence will manifest what is best for us according to their divine knowledge and universal law.

In some practices, this invitation may be directed to "the Lord and Lady" or specific deities like Isis and Osiris. Other traditions may focus solely on the Goddess, celebrating the divine feminine in its many forms.

To invite the Goddess and God into the circle, each covener can place their hands over their heart (body) and forehead (mind), and then extend their arms outward (spirit), saying:

I humbly invite the Goddess and God into circle – may you manifest in my body, mind, and spirit.

If your coven is dedicated to a particular deity, you may create a unique invitation to honor them. In my first coven, which was dedicated to Lilith, we used the following:

We honor thee Lilith
Winged Goddess of the dawn and night,
Bathe us in your dark light.
We witches gather in your sight,
Sharing your eternal flight.

These words became the lyrics of a song titled "Dark Goddess," featured on my 2024 re-release solo album called *Witch Web* (streaming on all platforms).

By inviting deities with reverence and respect, we open ourselves to their divine guidance and allow their wisdom to align with our intentions, trusting in the flow of universal energies to guide us toward what is truly meant to be.

Final thoughts

Crafting a sacred space and invoking the elements and deities are not just foundational practices in witchcraft - they are acts of devotion and connection. These rituals align your energy with the divine, ground your intentions, and magnify the power of your magick.

When you gather as a coven or community to prepare and work magick together, you amplify not only the energy of your intentions but also the collective force of the group. This shared effort creates a ripple effect that can extend beyond individual desires, weaving healing, transformation, and empowerment into the fabric of the collective consciousness, and even the world itself.

By collaborating and uniting your strengths, you create a force that is greater than the sum of its parts. This is the heart of coven work: to channel personal growth into collective empowerment and extend those blessings to the greater good.

Personalize these sacred practices so they resonate deeply with you and your community. Infuse them with meaning, passion, and authenticity, so your magickal efforts become a beacon of change, healing, and hope, reminding us that the energy we raise today shapes the world of tomorrow.

THE CIRCLE IS RIPE WITH POTENT ENERGIES . . . NOW WHAT?

Now that the Circle has been cast and is brimming with potent energies, it's time to perform the specific tasks, rituals, or spells you've prepared for this sacred space. While there is an element of theatre in ritual - the words, gestures, and their impact on those within the circle - it's crucial not to get lost in the role-playing. Focus on the feeling and intent behind your actions.

Simplify for success

A simple ritual performed with confidence and passion will pack a more powerful magickal punch than a complicated, disjointed performance. Remember the KISS principle: Keep It Simple Sorceress/er! As you gain experience, you can create more elaborate rituals, but in the beginning, simplicity is key.

Raising power

Spellcasting and ritual work often involve raising power to fuel the magickal transformation. The circle contains these energies, like arrows in a well-strung bow, ready to be released to do their work.

Cone of power

A cone of power is a spinning mass of energy built by the coveners to fuel spells. Music, chanting, drumming, running, or rhythmic breathing - all done passionately and with unified intent - can raise this cone of power.

Raising power through music and movement

- ★ MUSIC: Music is the voice of the soul and can be a powerful way to raise energy. Choose tracks that excite your coveners or perform the music together if you're musically inclined.
- ★ CHANTING: Chanting the names of your deities or a significant phrase can build energy. The "Wiccan Goddess Chant," for example, is a potent classic: *Isis, Astarte, Diana, Hecate, Demeter, Kali, Inanna.*
- ★ SINGING: Acapella singing of inspirational words can also raise power. Repeating a chorus from a favorite song with increasing intensity can be very effective.
- ★ DRUMMING: Drumming is a favorite for many witches. The rhythm and intensity of drumming can hypnotically raise an excellent cone of power.

- ★ **Breath toning:** Breathing in and out audibly, with a big "oooh" sound, can raise power. Be mindful to avoid hyperventilation.
- ★ **Physical movement:** Running around in a circle can be effective if space allows. This method is energetic and can be quite fun!

Releasing the power

Once raised, the power can be released in several ways. One method is to hold hands slightly aloft and, as the cone peaks, throw them to the sky while calling:

By one this spell is done,
By two it shall come true,
By three so mote it be,
By four for the good of all,
By five our dreams come ALIVE!

Visualize the circle parting overhead, creating a vortex that whisks the energy away to manifest your intent.

Alternatively, visualize the power spiraling out like smoke as you cut a large pentagram into the top of the circle with your athame. This releases the energy to do its work in the physical world.

Earthing the power

After raising and releasing power, you may feel residual energy in the circle. To ground this energy, place your hands on the ground and visualize the residue draining into the earth. Alternatively, stand and consciously channel it through your feet.

Opening the circle

Once your ritual or spellcasting is complete, it's time to open the circle. This is a moment to ground your energy, express gratitude, and return to the everyday world with balance and focus.

OPENING THE CIRCLE

You have created and worked within a magickal "container" - your Circle. When the work is complete it's time to "open" it and release the energies.:

1. **Thank the deities and elements:** Acknowledge and release the energies of the deities, elements, and directions you invoked during your ritual.
2. **Visualize the circle dissolving:** Imagine the protective energy of the circle gently receding into the earth or rising into the sky, returning to the universal energy.
3. **Ground yourself:** Share your cakes and ale mindfully, allowing the act of eating and drinking to ground any remaining energy. Reflect on the ritual's purpose and your gratitude for the magickal experience.

CAKES AND ALE

The "cakes and ale" ceremony is a traditional part of many witchcraft rituals. It is a symbolic act of sharing and gratitude, honoring the Goddess and God, as well as the energies raised during the ritual. The act of eating and drinking helps ground any excess energy, bringing you back to the physical plane while celebrating the abundance and blessings in your life.

Typically, the "cakes" can be anything from homemade bread or biscuits to simple store-bought treats. The "ale" traditionally refers to a small amount of wine, mead, or beer, but there are plenty of non-alcoholic alternatives: a refreshing herbal tea, sparkling juice, or even water infused with herbs or fruits can work beautifully. Choose options that feel sacred and meaningful to your practice.

Timing of cakes and ale

In your coven, you may choose to enjoy the cakes and ale ceremony either before or after formally opening the circle.

By incorporating cakes and ale into your practice, you add a grounding, celebratory element that completes your ritual with reverence and joy. Whether shared communally in a coven or quietly in solitary practice, this act honors the divine and reminds you of the sacredness in the everyday.

THANKING THE DEITIES

Acknowledging and thanking the deities invoked during your ritual is an important part of opening your circle. It shows respect for the divine forces that have assisted you and ensures balance and gratitude in your magickal practice. Whether you work with ancient gods and goddesses, archetypes, or universal energies, your words of thanks can be personalized to reflect the unique connection you've cultivated.

Here's an example of a release and thanks for Hecate:

Thank you, Hecate, Queen of the crossroads,
Greek goddess of the night,
For witnessing, blessing, and assisting our rite.
We bid you hail and farewell, until next in circle we dwell.

When addressing deities of different names and origins, you might incorporate aspects of their cultural significance or roles. For example:

★ *Thank you, Isis, great mother of magick, for your guidance and blessings.*
★ *Thank you, Odin, keeper of wisdom and runes, for sharing your insight and strength.*
★ *Thank you, Brigid, goddess of poetry and healing, for igniting inspiration and nurturing light.*

The key is to honor the specific energy you've called upon with words that feel meaningful and authentic.

HONOR THE DIVINITY WITHIN

After farewelling the deities, take a moment to reconnect with your own sacred power. Ground your energy and affirm your place as a channel of the divine:

I am sacred, I honor my divinity.
I thank the powers within and without for assisting and blessing me.

By honoring both the divine forces beyond and the sacred energy within, you complete your ritual in balance and gratitude, fully grounded in the power of your magick.

RELEASING THE ELEMENTS

Releasing the elements at the end of a ritual is a moment of gratitude and balance, acknowledging the energies that supported your magickal work. There are two ways to approach this:

1. Release each element individually: Face each quarter - east (air), south (fire or earth), west (water), and north (earth or fire) - and address each element by name. Use your athame (or finger) to trace a pentagram in the air as you release their energy, saying:

   We honor the element of [air/fire/water/earth] for your presence and assistance.
   Hail and farewell, until next in circle we dwell.

2. Group release in one statement: If you prefer a more fluid approach, you can release all the elements at once. Stand at the center of the circle, raise your athame, and trace a single pentagram, intoning:

   We honor the elements and their assistance.
   Hail and farewell, until next in circle we dwell.

Choose the method that feels most meaningful to you and your group. Whether you honor each element individually or as a collective, the act of releasing them with intention and gratitude ensures balance and closure, leaving the circle grounded and harmonious.

OPENING THE CIRCLE

Using your athame, trace an energy line at the edge of the sphere in a counterclockwise movement if in the north and clockwise if in the southern hemisphere, to disperse the circle, and say:

The circle is open but unbroken, carried within our hearts.
Always merry meet and always merry part.

WORDS MATTER

When opening a circle, the final words carry a special significance. One traditional statement often used is:

The circle is open but unbroken, carried within our hearts.
Always merry meet and always merry part.

This phrase is a beloved part of modern pagan and Wiccan practices. While its exact origin is unclear, it has become a cherished way to honor the enduring connection between those who gathered. The phrase "merry meet and merry part" reflects the joy of coming together and parting in harmony, while the unbroken circle symbolizes the continuity of the energy and intentions created during the ritual.

This simple yet powerful declaration captures the cyclical nature of the craft, reminding us that the bonds we create in ritual are carried forward, even as we return to the everyday world.

By following these steps, you ensure that your rituals are performed with respect, focus, and intention, making your magickal workings powerful and effective.

FEASTING

As noted in our Book of Shadows, *"Food and drink must always be consumed after circle to ground energies and enhance coveners' bonding in the physical realm."*

The importance of feasting

After performing magickal work, it's essential to ground yourself. Eating and drinking help "earth" the energies raised during the ritual. This process is crucial for several reasons:

- ★ Grounding energies: Intense magickal work can leave you feeling lightheaded or with a fluttering sensation in your stomach. Grounding through food and drink stabilizes your energy, making it easier to return to the everyday world.
- ★ Preventing restlessness: Without grounding, you might experience difficulty sleeping or have unsettling dreams. Consuming food and drink helps calm your energy, promoting restful sleep.
- ★ Bonding and reflection: Feasting provides an opportunity to chat and reflect on the ritual, strengthening the bond between coven members. However, avoid discussing specific spells to allow them to manifest without interference.

Types of feasts

- ★ Sabbat celebrations: During Sabbats, spend ample time eating, drinking, and enjoying each other's company. These gatherings are longer and more festive.
- ★ Full moon gatherings or specific rituals: Typically, these involve a simpler fare, such as tea and cookies. Always offer a portion of your food and drink to the Goddess, either directly on the earth or by collecting crumbs and drink for libations later.

CHECKLIST FOR COVEN MEETING

1. Plan the gathering: Determine the purpose, date, and time of the meeting. Is it a full moon ritual, a Sabbat celebration, or a spellcasting session? Define your intent clearly.

2. Coordinate with coven members: Use a group chat, email, or a scheduling app to confirm everyone's availability and attendance. Ensure clear communication about the plan.
3. Select a location: Choose a safe, accessible, and private space. Whether it's someone's home, a sacred outdoor site, or a rented venue, ensure it suits the purpose of the gathering.
4. Prepare ritual details: Outline the purpose and structure of the ritual. Share suggested tools, attire, and any chants or invocations ahead of time so everyone is prepared and aligned with the intent.
5. Gather supplies: Collect or purchase any specific ingredients or tools needed for the ritual or spells. Consider sustainability by using natural or reusable materials when possible.
6. Set up the space: On the day of the meeting, create a sacred environment. Arrange the altar, mark the circle if desired, and ensure the area is cleansed and ready for magickal work.
7. Cast the circle: Create a protected and empowered space by casting the circle with intention. This marks the beginning of the formal ritual and holds the energy of your working.
8. Invite and honor deities and invoke the elements: Invite any deities, guides, or spiritual allies you wish to work with. Welcome the elemental energies at the four directions to support and empower the ritual.
9. Perform the ritual: Carry out the ceremony, spell, or rite as planned. Follow the structure discussed and agreed upon with the group, while allowing space for intuitive flow if needed.
10. Thank and release deities and guides: Offer gratitude to the spiritual presences you invited in. Acknowledge their

support and respectfully release them from the space, trusting that their blessings continue with you.

11. Release the elements: Dismiss the elemental energies with appreciation. This honors their role in the rite and creates neutral balance in the space.
12. Open the circle: Open the circle, dispersing the sacred space and grounding any remaining energy. Ensure that all participants feel fully present.
13. Celebrate together: Share food, drinks, and meaningful conversation to ground energies and strengthen your connection as a coven. This time together is an essential part of bonding and integrating the ritual's energy.

FINAL THOUGHTS

Your first coven gathering doesn't have to be stressful and overwhelming. Likewise, coven gatherings don't have to become perfunctory or repetitive. Always think about what you are all doing, be creative, and trust in your coven's magickal potential. This will ensure that your covenworld evolves to be always lush, challenging, and exciting.

CHAPTER 8

DEDICATE YOUR COVEN

Your first coven gathering is likely to be the dedication of your coven. It's not essential to do this right away; in fact, you might prefer to have a couple of "practice sessions" before holding the important dedication ceremony. For example, in my coven, our first gathering was in front of television cameras! This may sound like exhibitionism, but it was actually for a good reason. At the time, I was pitching a television show in America about real-life witchcraft. I wanted to film an authentic gathering of witches performing a ritual, and my new coven members agreed to do a trial run in front of the cameras.

It's kind of bizarre having your first coven meeting in front of television cameras. Here are some glimpses of the experience from the diary I kept back in September 2002.

> *. . . For the ritual, we performed a banishing spell for Tri on someone who didn't understand her need for privacy. She was fed up, and we agreed it would be appropriate to banish the person "for the good of all, with harm to none." This way, we wouldn't interfere with their free will but create an energetic path for them to move on.*
>
> *The looks on the director's and cameraman's faces were priceless when we pulled out a red candle shaped like a naked figure and lit it, proclaiming, "We banish you from bothering Tri, for the good of all, this is our decree!" The energy felt potent . . . , and when Lupita played her accordion with long, slow, sensual notes, Tri and I swayed in unison as we chanted. The TV crew swayed too.*

The TV crew later commented on how thought-provoking and sensible our approach to witchcraft was, especially when we spoke about respecting the earth and working with its energies. One crew member admitted he had goosebumps during the spell, realizing that experiencing something magickal firsthand was powerful and eye-opening.

. . . a few weeks later, I asked Tri about the banishing spell. She said she had burned the candle, buried the remains, and hadn't been bothered since. Nothing negative came of the spell, so it seems it helped the other person move on with their life as well.

The planning, preparation, and actual ceremony were great practice for our forthcoming Mabon ceremony to dedicate the coven.

A GLIMPSE INTO THE PAST

In 2002, we dedicated the Dark Light of Lilith Coven.

It was an unforgettable night, and I want to share it with you in the hope that it inspires your own magickal path. I followed my heart, trusted my intuition, and together we created a ritual that was uniquely ours - intimate, powerful, and deeply meaningful.

Finding the right place had proven tricky, until a friend offered her home in the Hollywood Hills. She was renovating and had a vast rooftop balcony with panoramic views of Los Angeles and the endless sky above. It was perfect - especially under the light of the Mabon full harvest moon which bathed everything in its silvery glow.

The day of the ritual was a chaotic dash around esoteric shops gathering everything we needed, including a wolf's heart sealed in a pewter canister. When the sun finally set, I dressed in black: a simple dress layered with a thick wool coat and knee-high boots. I was weighed down with bags - candles, incense, a large cauldron, and a camera to capture the moment.

Tri, Lupita, and I made our way to the rooftop. The lights of Los Angeles sparkled below like a carpet of stars. We immediately began laying a circle of tea lights and preparing the altar. The moon crested the ridge just minutes before 8:55 PM - her full moment. We quickly lit the candles and completed the setup.

We were ready.

I raised my arms, athame pointed high, and cast the circle. We'd rehearsed earlier, so our movements flowed in sync. The energy was strong - solid and bright, encircling us like a living web. I imagined my blade catching strands of moonlight, weaving them into a luminous cocoon of protection and power.

With the circle cast, Tri lit our coven candle - a thick black pillar in an ornate pewter base. It would only be lit again during our sacred gatherings, when invoking our patron goddess, Lilith.

Together, we called her name. As our voices blended, I could see them in my mind's eye - swirling like incense smoke, spiraling into a passage through which her essence could join us. The air thickened; I felt breathless, sensing her presence. Lupita and Tri felt it too, and we spoke our coven creed aloud.

We each made our personal commitment to the coven - what we hoped to bring, to learn, and to offer - in perfect love and perfect trust. Then, we declared to all the worlds, seen and unseen, that the Dark Light of Lilith Coven now existed.

Lupita sprinkled incense over the glowing charcoal in the cauldron, and one by one we passed items from our personal shrines through the fragrant smoke, consecrating them in the name of our coven. Last to be blessed was our Book of Shadows, which I placed carefully on the altar as we prepared for the blood offering.

With a quill and dragon's blood ink, I wrote the first letter of my name. Then I pricked my finger and pressed my blood beside it. Tri and Lupita did the same. We cut strands of our hair and bound them together, sealing them in the pewter canister with the wolf's heart - our totem animal, symbol of strength, cunning, and fierce devotion.

With all blessed and bonded, we raised power. I had gathered a sequence of ancient words, researched and woven together for use only in our circle. As we chanted, the energy intensified - building, pulsing, alive. The words rose louder and louder, echoing off the hill behind us. At the peak of the power, we threw our arms to the sky and cried out: "Lilith! Lilith! Lilith!"

A sudden wind surged around us. I felt our raised energy swept up and carried to the edges of the world. Then, we dropped to our knees and placed our hands on the rooftop to earth it all back into the ground.

Afterward, I grabbed my Instamatic camera, and before selfies were a thing, I stretched my arm out and snapped a photo of the three of us - hugging, breathless, and forever changed.

An hour and a half after arriving, we left that rooftop transformed. We stopped at a café on Sunset Boulevard to ground ourselves with tea and cookies, still feeling deeply connected and excited for the future of our coven.

In the days that followed, we knew we had done something important. Creating such a formal and elaborate ritual had been exactly what we needed to begin our journey together - anchored in intention, unity, and magick.

PLANNING YOUR DEDICATION

Good planning and preparation are essential for making the event powerful and magickal. Here is a guide for planning your own coven dedication.

1. Decide to hold the gathering.
2. Communicate with coven members: Ensure everyone's attendance via email or phone.
3. Choose a location: Select an accessible, private, safe, and secure venue.
4. Prepare ritual details: Write or copy the purpose and outline of the ritual, including suggested magickal tools and appropriate attire. Share these details with each covener.
5. Gather ingredients: Buy or gather specific ingredients needed for spells or the ritual.
6. Prepare the space: On the day of the meeting, set up the altar and create a physical demarcation of the circle if desired.

Performing the coven meeting

1. Cast the circle: Create a sacred space by casting the circle.
2. Call on the elements: Invoke the energies of air, fire, water, and earth.
3. Honor the Goddess and God: Acknowledge their presence within the coveners and invite a specific deity if appropriate.
4. Perform the ritual: Conduct the planned ritual or spellcasting.
5. Raise a cone of power: Build and release energy to fuel the spell or ritual.

6. **Ground residual energy:** Place hands on the ground or channel energy through the soles of your feet to ground any leftover power.
7. **Thank and farewell the deities:** Thank and farewell any specific deities invited, and honor the Goddess and God within.
8. **Release the elements:** Formally release the elemental energies.
9. **Open the circle:** Disperse the energy line and open the circle.
10. **Feast:** Eat, drink, and enjoy each other's company to ground energies and enhance bonding.

By creating a plan like this, your coven dedication can be a memorable and magickal experience for all involved.

Checklist for coven dedication

1. Decide on ethics and responsibilities and compile them in a list.
2. Decide on your initial gathering days: It's a good idea in the early stages to agree, for example, that every Thursday night you will meet for coffee and a chat about how the coven is progressing, then that every Sunday night you will do a ritual for the first two months. This will help you build up familiarity and confidence with magickal proceedings. As time goes on, you may agree to only physically meet on Esbats (full moon gatherings), special necessary events (like healing rituals and required spellcastings), and Sabbats. Of course, every morning when you perform your morning dedication you are psychically meeting with your coven members on the astral planes in your covenworld.
3. Write your coven creed: This should be an evocative piece that states the magickal purpose of the coven and celebrates the patron god/dess in a way that each coven member can personally identify with.
4. Write the invocation of your god/dess: These are the words to be used when venerating and inviting their presence in the circle.
5. Write your coven's own power-raising chant: As I've mentioned, I researched ancient words and names related to the story of Lilith and created a unique chant that only the Dark Light of Lilith Coven members know and use.
6. Decide on coven ritual structures and procedures: For example, the methods of casting a circle and performing invocations so that everyone can learn them. These will be copied into your Book of Shadows.

7. Establish home shrines to act as a personal doorway to your covenworld: I have two altars at home, one for my general personal magick, and one representing my coven membership - it is in front of this altar that I perform my morning dedication. As a group we agreed on certain objects relating to Lilith that our shrines would need to include: a black candle, an agate cave crystal (as I've mentioned, legend says she lived in a cave when she left the Garden of Eden), a small mirror (again, Lilith is also said to live in mirrors), and an image of an owl - a night bird of wisdom and related to Lilith in her winged aspect. We also agreed that our coven totem, the wolf heart, would initially stay on my shrine but would be shared around equally, staying at each of our homes. When you are deciding what should be included in your home shrines, be guided by what your god/goddess holds sacred and be as creative as you like.
8. Write a coven member blessing: I also created a coven member blessing that is standard and can be used from covener to covener as an acknowledgment and blessing within the circle. Ours goes:

> [*Name*], *I honor you as witch of the Dark Light of Lilith Coven.*
> *May you always grow ever stronger and more powerful*
> *In heart, mind, spirit, and magick.*

9. Create a morning dedication: a morning dedication is an important affirmation of magickal intent. It also works to align the astral and psychic energies of the coveners between the worlds in the sacred space of the covenworld. You can write a dedication together using ours as a guideline if you like:

Sample morning dedication

Light your altar candle and incense. Close your eyes, breathe deeply, center, and focus within. Meditate on "the green" - the calm, still place that exists within where your spirit dwells beyond the realm of everyday experience. With the index finger of your power hand (the one you write with), perform the pentagram salute - like the sign of the cross that Christians use but touching third eye (between eyebrows), then right breast, left shoulder, right shoulder, left breast, third eye again. Then say:

In perfect love and perfect trust
I dedicate myself to the universal forces of magick
And declare myself witch of the [*coven name*].

10. Choose the location and time of the coven dedication.
11. Write up the ritual outline and agree on appropriate attire.
12. Make a list of all objects required and go shopping if necessary.
13. Make the appropriate incense if you like and choose your coven totem.

COVEN TOTEM

A coven totem is an object that symbolizes the power of your coven. It can be empowered and act as a conduit for the coven's unique energy and magick. We chose a wolf's heart, but you could choose just about anything that holds symbolic meaning to you: an eagle feather, a shark tooth, a beautiful crystal, an ancient fossil . . . whatever you like. Keep it in a special container and put something physical from each coven member and any new coven member in there with it (hair is usually the best). In this way you are bound together and empowered by what the object represents.

STEPS FOR A COVEN DEDICATION RITUAL

1. Shower/bathe with intent to purify, and dress in ritual attire.
2. Gather at the chosen location.
3. Prepare the altar and, if preferred, physically mark out the circle.
4. Cast the circle.
5. Invoke your patron god/dess.
6. State the coven creed.
7. Have each covener verbally confirm their commitment to the coven and discuss the importance of personal supportive coven practice as well as group gatherings to maintain the existence of the covenworld.
8. Bless and consecrate all coven and personal objects of magick (we did this by passing each object through specially blended incense smoke).
9. Write coveners' names and make offerings of blood in coven Book of Shadows to seal intent.
10. Empower the coven totem (we did this by cutting and binding our hair together and placing it in the canister with the wolf's heart).
11. Raise power to announce the existence of the coven and to kickstart the covenworld.
12. Ground any energy raised by placing hands on ground.
13. Open the circle.
14. Eat together and further ground energy.
15. Go home, have interesting dreams, and wake up as an empowered member of your coven!

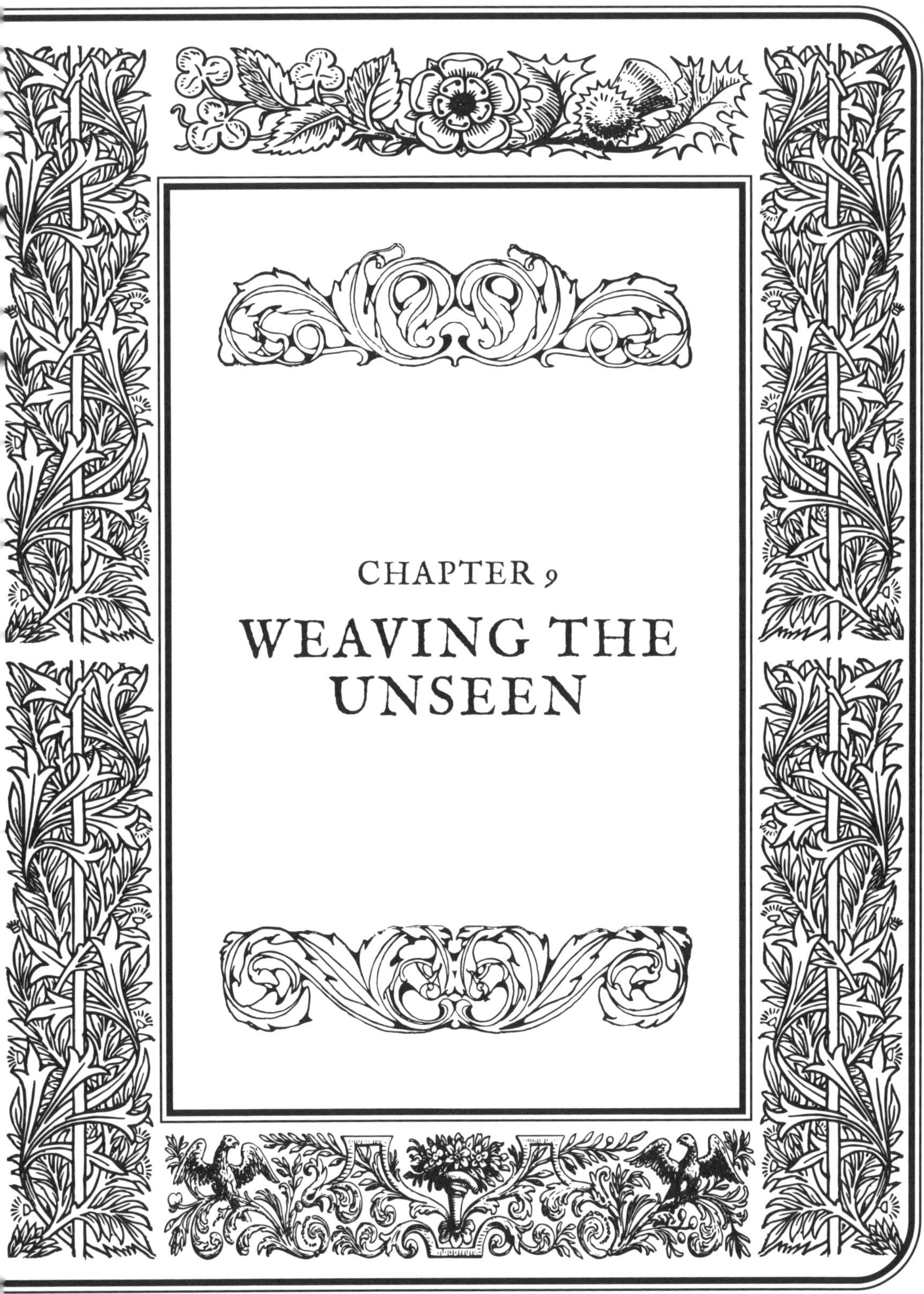

CHAPTER 9

WEAVING THE UNSEEN

An essential part of developing as a coven is aligning psychically with one another. A well-formed covenworld is more than just an idea; it becomes a living, vibrant entity on the astral plane, working continuously to protect, support, and empower each member. The beauty of a strong covenworld is that it operates even when you're not consciously focusing on it, acting as an energetic anchor for your group.

To manifest a truly effective covenworld, honing your group meditation and visualization skills is vital. These practices not only strengthen your collective energy but also enhance your ability to cast circles, raise power, and perform spells with precision and potency.

GROUP MEDITATION

Group meditation doesn't need to be complicated to be powerful. It can be as simple as sitting in a circle, holding hands, and focusing on a shared color or intention. Alternatively, it can involve more structured approaches, such as guided imagery, synchronized breathing, or specific body positions designed to amplify energy.

Here are a few accessible and effective disciplines to practice together:

1. Unified visualization: Choose a single image, symbol, or color to focus on, and work together to hold it in your minds. This creates a shared mental space that strengthens your psychic connection.
2. Breath alignment: Sit together and synchronize your breathing, inhaling and exhaling as one. This not only harmonizes your energy but also fosters a sense of unity and calm.
3. Energy linking: Visualize a thread of light connecting each member of the group, forming a web of energy. This thread represents your shared intentions and the bond of your covenworld.
4. Shared intention meditation: As a group, choose a collective goal or intention. Meditate on this together, visualizing it as already achieved, and allow the group's energy to infuse the vision with power.

These practices are not just exercises - they are acts of creation. By committing to them, you build a foundation for your coven that is strong, resilient, and deeply magickal. The benefits extend far beyond your ritual space, enriching both your collective practice and your individual lives.

Discipline 1

Stand together in a circle with the tips of your Saturn finger (the middle finger) touching the Saturn finger of the covener next to you. Synchronize your breathing so that you are gently inhaling and exhaling together. See everyone's conjoined breath blend together in the center and be aware that you are breathing in the air that has been in your covenmates' lungs - you are all intimately connected in this way. You will probably feel a spontaneous cone of power start to whiz through and around you as your breath becomes increasingly charged with your unified intent. Stay in the moment for as long as you can until one person (chosen before the ritual begins) speaks out: "*Now unified as one, our coven's work is done.*" All deeply inhale the energy that has built up, open your eyes, and drop your hands to the floor to earth any excess energy. Sit and discuss your thoughts and impressions, writing up anything important in your Book of Shadows.

Discipline 2

Color is not only a potent and familiar thing to psychically project, but it is also healing and balancing. The following meditation is effective for group consciousness raising.

Lie opposite each other with feet touching sole to sole. Agree on which person starts, then close your eyes and take some deep breaths together. The agreed-on person then starts to send the color.

First they picture it forming like a cloud or a pool of liquid in their head before seeing it floating or streaming down their bodies to run into the other person. The color is sent like this until someone who has been appointed as the timer says "*It is done.*" Then the meditators open their eyes and the person receiving the color describes which color it was they were visualizing. You will find that 90 percent of the time they will be correct, but this success rate will depend on how confident and powerful the meditator is. Then the meditation is reversed with the other person receiving the color. In an unevenly numbered coven everyone rotates until all have had a go.

Discipline 3

Sit together with your arms stretched out to either side with the tips of your Saturn (middle) fingers touching. Together imagine that a presence is supporting your arms. This is not a spirit presence that you are invoking, just a sensation of support. This arm position is difficult to maintain under normal consciousness; however, with the coven psychically linked and visualizing support, it becomes effortless and you can hold it for five minutes or more. Try it and see! When you understand how combined intent can support and help you bear physical hardship, you will understand how to apply that collective energy to healing spells and rituals that you do for each other and anyone else in need.

Discipline 4

You may find it helpful to record these instructions as an audio guide for your group meditation. Use your phone, a voice recorder, or any device that allows you to create and replay the meditation easily.

Lie in a circle with your heads touching and your bodies extended outward like the spokes of a wheel. Where your heads meet, visualize a sphere of purple or violet light appearing and gently pulsing. See this light expand, gradually shifting to a shimmering white circle that envelops you all.

Imagine this wheel of light beginning to spin, with your bodies as its spokes. In the northern hemisphere, visualize it spinning sunwise (clockwise), and in the southern hemisphere, see it spinning counterclockwise.

As the light spins faster, you may collectively feel as if your bodies are lifting from the ground. Some participants might experience a spontaneous out-of-body sensation, feeling light and free as the energy flows.

Stay in this meditative state for at least 15 minutes. At the end, having a pre-recorded or spoken prompt can guide the group to completion. The phrase *"As above, so below; as the universe, so the soul"* can be spoken by one person or in unison, signaling the wheel to slow down.

Once the wheel comes to rest, say *"Grounded are we in body and spirit - unified, strong, and infinite."* This serves as a cue for everyone to open their eyes gently.

To ground any excess energy, roll over onto your stomachs and rest your foreheads on the floor. Take a few deep breaths, allowing the energy to settle back into the earth. Once grounded, relax and share your experiences as a group. Be sure to record any significant impressions in your Book of Shadows for future reflection.

These practices will psychically align and connect you, strengthening your collective focus and resilience. A united coven, working in harmony, can become a powerful force for positive transformation - both within your own lives and in the lives of others.

Once you have refined your group skills in psychic meditation, you can explore the following activities to deepen your connection and amplify your magickal impact.

Dream triggers

This one is good if you are away together on a retreat and sleeping in the same place, or if you have a good couple of days off from work or school, as it involves disturbing your sleep repeatedly throughout the night!

Go to bed with an alarm clock and phone next to your bed. Set the alarm to go off at an agreed time, waking you up. Then call each other on the phone (or speak if you are sleeping in the same space), say a specific word (the dream trigger), and then go back to sleep.

Another way to achieve this without calling or speaking to each other is to agree on a list of words and then read and visualize a word from the list at each alarm call.

For example, you all agree on a list of words: green, ocean, wolf. Next, ascertain that you will all likely be asleep by (for example) midnight, so the first alarm will be set for 1.30 am, the second at 3.30 am, and the third at 5 am. When you wake up with each alarm, say the word out loud, then visualize the word, set the alarm for the next agreed time, and go back to sleep. Repeat this for the remaining words and alarm times.

Upon waking, you all immediately write your dream recollections down in a dream diary (a book especially used for dream recall and analysis) and then compare your dreams at the next gathering.

Profound insights can be achieved for ideas for rituals and other coven practices. It is quite likely that you will appear in each other's dreams. Make sure you keep a detailed record.

A good way to prepare for this dream trigger work is to each individually keep a dream diary for two weeks beforehand so that you get used to recalling your dreams. Just keep the book and a pen next to your bed and on waking write down anything you remember straight away. It doesn't matter if it seems like gobbledygook, just capture whatever recollections you have. When you analyze it later you will see patterns appear - and undoubtedly some revelations will come with the recognition of these patterns!

Astral traveling

Astral traveling is when a person's spirit leaves their body and either travels through the physical world that the body is inhabiting or shifts between the realms and travels in other realities.

My personal experience was that I would begin by meditating on nothing or nothingness. This is what my hypnotist prescribed for me to do for 20 minutes every morning and night during the treatment. "Nothing" or "nothingness" is a black, silent, emotionless state of zero. But from nothing comes something: as I hovered in the absolute nil of the moment I would also be contemplating the fecund potential of this state. When I fully grasped this, I would get an intense pressure in my third eye area (between my eyebrows) and then feel myself "lift" - in some ways it was more like movement outwards in every direction; not so much elevating, but expanding beyond my skin. The recollections I had immediately after my astral travels were less a stream of connected images and more like feelings that in one minute I would be in the room next door, the next out on the street, and so on.

As I did it more often I would really make an effort to notice details of my surroundings and then go back in my waking hours the next day and check if my recollections were correct. Quite a few times the tangible memories I had, like a freshly bloomed red flower in a garden next door or a new band flyer stuck to a pole down the street, were indeed correct.

The more abstract qualities of my traveling between the worlds had more to do with colors, light or the absence of it, and funnily enough sensory events - a smoky smell and a metallic taste in the back of my throat. I wrote the recollections of these astral journeys in my Book of Shadows and the recurring theme of my travels was that they were insights into the nature of existence and spirit as permeating all things, and time being an illusion - like the song lyric I once wrote: "linear time - it's a wonderful lie."

To astral travel as a coven and attempt to meet outside of your bodies, here is an exercise you may find helpful.

Agree on a specific location. Place a physical representation of yourselves there to help draw your spirits: some hair from each of you entwined and placed in a container with a clear quartz crystal and buried or hidden in the location is a good way of ensuring you all navigate your way there successfully. You could perhaps all decide that you are going to meditate at exactly 11 pm and "meet" at the spot where your homing signal is buried. Then perform the following ritual at the appointed time.

A RITUAL FOR ASTRAL TRAVELING

Note: This ritual is for those who are seeking to develop the skill of astral traveling. Those who can do it spontaneously can skip these instructions and just get straight to it!

Burn some incense of nutmeg, or if you can't get this as incense buy it as an essential oil and drop about five drops on water in an oil burner. Nutmeg will assist your consciousness to leave your body. Sit comfortably upright (don't lie down - you'll probably fall asleep!) with your back resting against a wall, your legs straight out in front of you and your palms in your lap. Breathe deeply and let your body feel heavy like lead. If any thoughts enter your mind acknowledge them and then visualize them floating away: in and out they come and go, like your breath, in and out, in and out.

Now take your awareness to your third eye (between your eyebrows) and see a spark of light there. See everything around it grow dark as that spark becomes the concentrated essence of you. You are that spark: see your spirit body take shape and form from the spark. When it is glowing very bright, see it leap out of your forehead and hover in the air. Now, look back at your physical body resting upright against the wall. In your spirit form start to travel to the agreed meeting location. You may find that this feels like you are "imagining" walking out your front door and down the street. Imagining is fine, because it is the integral step to "doing it." The shift from you imagining to you astral traveling is very subtle and you may not even realize it has occurred.

When you "arrive" at the agreed meeting place look around and see who else is there. For the first few times don't attempt to communicate by normal physical methods, just relax and see what happens. After a couple of "meetings" like this, you will find that conversations and activities will start to flow - in fact, all sorts of things will start to happen!

When you feel it is time, return back to your body the same way you left it. You might find that you spontaneously appear in front of your body rather than walking back like the way you left. The main thing is that when you see your body in front of you, shrink yourself back to the spark of light and enter back through the third eye of your physical body.

Stay resting there for a moment and really experience the sensation of being back in your physical body. Wiggle your fingers and your toes, stretch a little, and slowly open your eyes. Give yourself a massage; rub your arms and legs, belly, back, and head to awaken all your physical self. Then write down all your recollections and compare them with those of your covenmates.

The first few times, you may feel you are controlling the journey by imagining every step of it, but this will change, and one day you will find there is a lot of stuff going on that you are not initiating. The important thing when this happens is to have the ritual of returning to your body highly familiarized so that you can always get back no matter what. Sometimes having a key word can be a good idea. If you are surfing the astral planes and you don't like where you are, you can state the key word and it will immediately bring you back to standing in front of your body. Sometimes a silvery cord of light attaches to the physical self. But it is not always there, and that's why I think a key word is a very good thing to have as a backup to always find your way home.

To set a key word, go into the meditation as described above but when you have the spark of self ignited in your third eye, instead of casting it forward to leave your body, keep your awareness focused within your third eye. Now say the word at least 20 times, either out loud or silently. As you do this, fully comprehend that this word is the key that transcends all boundaries and will immediately make your physical body accessible to your spirit no matter what. By the way, the key word can be as elaborate as you like - it can even be a word you make up. The only requisite is that it is only known to you. It is best to keep your key word private even from other coven members.

Astral traveling gets easier the more you do it, and when you share the experience as part of a coven ritual the tangibility and clarity of the experience will be enhanced. Keep a record of what you experience and any insights gained, as these will be valuable tools to assist you in the development of your craft.

COVEN DEDICATIONS

You will be performing your coven dedications every morning, but you can also do it at other times during the day, synchronized with your covenmates. For example, agree to do the dedications every hour from 5 to 11 pm for one week. At the precise time, spend two minutes performing the dedication and thinking of your coven members. Repeated affirmations of your connection with each other will create powerful psychic links.

GROUP SPELLS

There are so many books on spellcasting, both solitary and in groups, including my dedicated spellbook, the *Lost Book of Spells*.

In additional to spell and ritual work, I would suggest coven members become adept at "charging". This is the coven projecting your combined focused will to empower an object, person, or even event.

Charging ritual

1. Cast the circle as usual.
2. Place the object to be empowered in the center of the circle, either on the altar, on a table, or wherever - just make sure it is in the center and can be seen and focused on by everyone. The object can be your combined coven jewelry, a photo of a person who needs healing (or the person themself!), or a written description of an upcoming event that you want to bless.
3. All together, touch your fingers of Saturn (the middle finger) with the next person and breathe in unison. Whoever is leading the ritual then says the following:

    For the good of all with harm to none,
    Our power is great, our work's begun.

4. All visualize a beam of light leaving your individual third eye chakras and see them fuse together as a ball of light around the object or person being charged. You will likely feel tingles all over, as you not only power up the object but power up each other. When it is obvious the power is peaking, the leader says:

    For the good of all with harm to none,
    Our power is great, our work is done.

5. On "done," everyone exhales together and says:

    So mote it be.

6. This seals the charge, and the object, person, or event is empowered.
7. Next, it is a good idea for the coveners to place their hands on the floor and earth any excess power. The charging ritual can then be completed by opening the circle as normal.

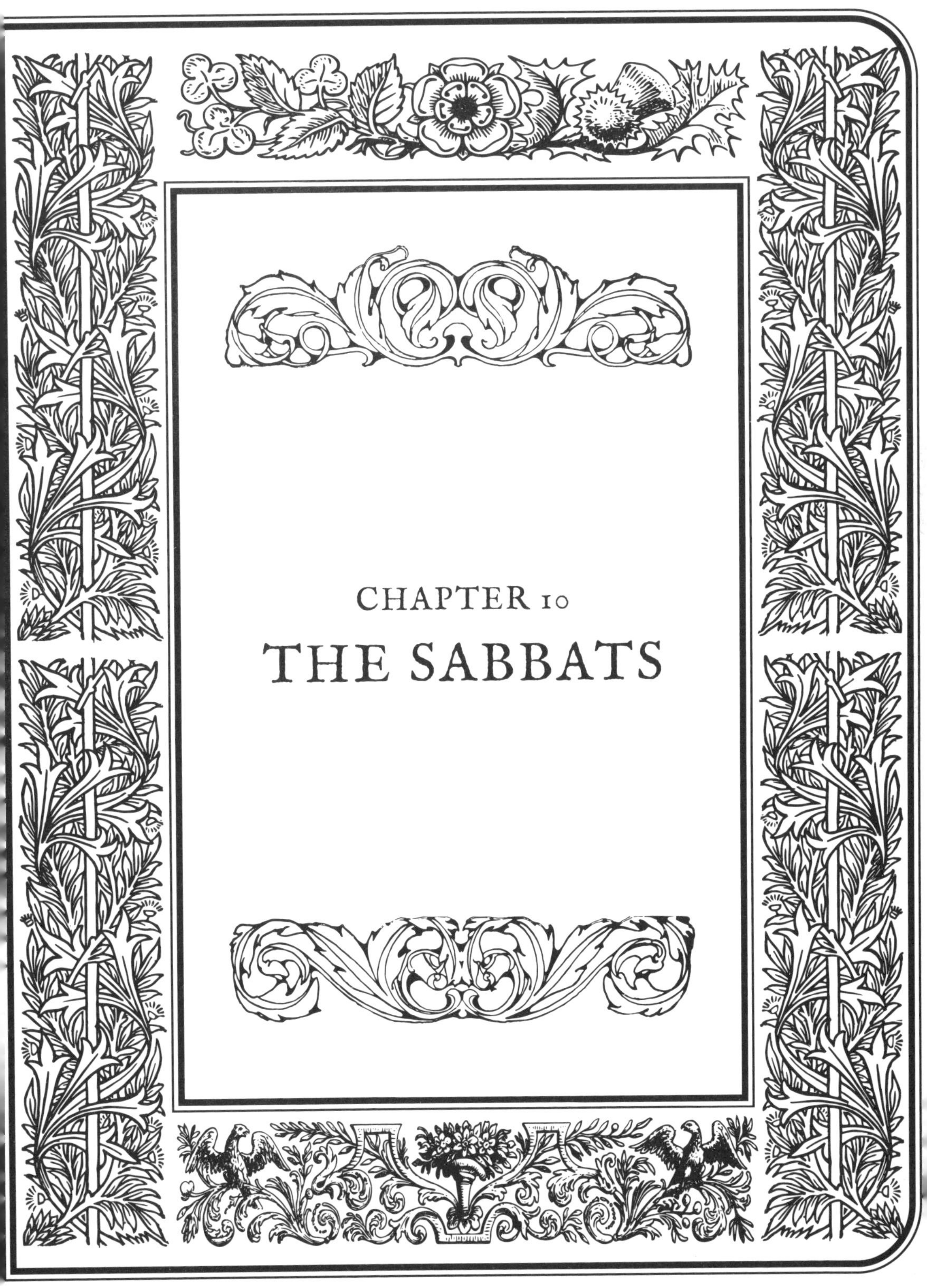

CHAPTER 10

THE SABBATS

The Sabbats are witchcraft's holy days, similar to Christmas for Christians, Ramadan for Muslims, and Hanukkah for Jews. There are eight Sabbats, spaced roughly six weeks apart throughout the year, corresponding to agricultural and astronomical events. This cycle is known as the Wheel of the Year. Turning the wheel honors and respects the cycles of destruction, death, decay, birth, growth, and renewal in both the material and spiritual worlds.

While I have written extensively about the Sabbats in my earliest books - *Witch: a Personal Journey, Witch: a Magickal Year*, and more recently in *Teen Magick,* I want to offer a concise reference guide here.

A NOTE ON SABBATS IN THE SOUTHERN HEMISPHERE

Since the Sabbats are seasonal, they are opposite in the southern hemisphere compared to the northern hemisphere. The Greater Sabbats (Samhain, Imbolc, Beltane, and Lammas) are based on the agricultural cycles of northern Europe and have been revived in modern Wiccan/pagan tradition. The four Lesser Sabbats are the solstices and equinoxes.

SAMHAIN

- ★ **Date:** October 31 (northern hemisphere), May 1 (southern hemisphere).
- ★ **Land:** The final storing of food for winter, a clear indication that winter is coming.
- ★ **Life:** The ending and the beginning - a festival of death is celebrated. It is a time when the veil between the spirit world and the material world lifts, allowing those departed to join those still living.
- ★ **Altar items:** Black candles, apples, pomegranates, and carved pumpkins.
- ★ **Ritual theme:** Honoring and contacting the spirits of departed loved ones.
- ★ **Coven activity:** A journey to honor and remember. Gather your coven for a meaningful experience to honor Samhain's themes of remembrance, connection, and reflection.
    - » **Visit a cemetery together:** Choose a cemetery with historical or personal significance. As you walk through the grounds, reflect on the lives of those who have passed, leaving small offerings like flowers, herbs, or stones as tokens of respect.
    - » **Create a remembrance altar:** Once at the cemetery or another outdoor space, set up a temporary altar. Include items that symbolize the season - apples, pomegranates, and black candles - along with photos, mementos, or the names of loved ones.
    - » **Silent reflection or sharing:** Sit in a circle and take a moment of silence to honor those who have crossed the veil. Optionally, invite coven members to share memories, stories, or messages they feel inspired to offer.
    - » **Picnic of remembrance:** Enjoy a mindful meal together, incorporating foods that symbolize the cycle of life and death. Apples, bread, and seasonal fruits can represent life's sweetness and abundance, while pomegranates embody transformation and the underworld. This picnic can serve as a celebration of life and a way to ground the spiritual energy of the day.
    - » **Guided group meditation:** Conclude your visit with a group meditation or visualization. Imagine the spirits of loved ones

gathering peacefully, offering wisdom, comfort, and love. Envision the veil lifting momentarily to allow this connection before gently settling back into place.

» **Release and gratitude:** Before leaving, thank the spirits for their presence and the land for holding space. Leave your altar items or biodegradable offerings as a final token of gratitude.

- **Additional ideas for Samhain:**

  » **Memory lanterns:** Create lanterns with designs or words that honor loved ones and light them during your gathering.

  » **Seasonal crafting:** Make wreaths or garlands from autumn leaves and herbs to decorate your altar or home.

  » **Ancestral research:** Spend time as a coven exploring familial or local histories, connecting to the stories of those who came before.

YULE (WINTER SOLSTICE)

- **Date:** December 20-23 (northern hemisphere), June 20-23 (southern hemisphere).
- **Land:** The longest night before the sun is born anew and begins its ascent to summer.
- **Life:** A witch's Christmas and a time to burn the Yule log (slow-burning wood) and honor the belief that from death comes life.
- **Altar items:** Gold candles, mistletoe, and pine cones.
- **Ritual theme:** Celebrate friendship, companionship, and abundance.
- **Coven activity:** A joyous celebration of light and renewal. Gather your coven for a festive and meaningful celebration to honor the turning of the Wheel of the Year and the rebirth of the sun.

  » **Decorate a Yule altar together:** Begin the evening by creating a vibrant altar adorned with symbols of Yule. Include gold candles to represent the returning light, mistletoe for protection and love, and pine cones or evergreen branches for resilience and renewal. Invite each covener to contribute an item that symbolizes what they wish to manifest in the coming year.

» Burn the Yule log: Choose a log of slow-burning wood and decorate it with symbols of your intentions, such as ribbons or carvings. During the ritual, light the log as a group and share a moment of reflection. As the log burns, visualize releasing what no longer serves you and welcoming new opportunities with the reborn sun. If a fire isn't possible, a large gold candle can be used as a symbolic Yule log.
» Host a hearty feast: Prepare a communal feast featuring warm, hearty dishes such as casseroles, root vegetables, spiced puddings, and traditional mulled wine or cider. Incorporate seasonal flavors like cinnamon, cloves, and orange to evoke the spirit of Yule. Encourage coven members to contribute a dish or drink to share, enhancing the sense of abundance and community.
» Exchange gifts with intention: Exchange small, meaningful gifts that reflect the season's themes of renewal and joy. Each gift can include a handwritten note or blessing for the recipient, encouraging positivity and connection in the coming year.
» Candlelit vigil to welcome the sun: Stay up through the longest night, lighting candles to honor the returning sun. Create a sacred, serene space where coven members can reflect, meditate, or share their hopes for the new year. As dawn approaches, step outside to greet the first light together, symbolizing the sun's rebirth and the promise of brighter days ahead.
» Seasonal crafting: Make natural ornaments or charms together using materials like dried orange slices, cinnamon sticks, and ribbons. These can be kept as personal talismans or used to decorate your altar or home.

- Additional ideas for Yule:
    - Storytelling by the fire: Share myths and legends about the Winter Solstice, such as the rebirth of the sun or the Oak King and Holly King. Invite each covener to tell a favorite seasonal story.
    - Seasonal gratitude circle: Take turns sharing what you're grateful for from the past year and what you're excited to welcome in the year ahead.
    - Outdoor offering: If possible, take a moment to leave a small biodegradable offering outdoors as thanks to the earth for her gifts and a blessing for her renewal.

IMBOLC

- Date: February 1 (northern hemisphere), August 1 (southern hemisphere).
- Land: New life awakens, buds appear on trees and plants, and animals start to mate.
- Life: Cleanse your emotions by releasing old grudges and hang-ups; awaken the creative spirit by embarking on a new hobby like playing an instrument or making jewelry.
- Altar items: A corn dolly, representing the sacred goddess of this time - Brigid - surrounded by white candles and red blossoms.
- Ritual theme: Purification, transformation, and new beginnings; a sacred time for women and the arts. The promise of spring means the awakening of the maiden - a time for recharging the divine feminine within. Her warming breath heals the land and our hearts from the winter cold, promising new energies and approaching abundance.
- Coven activity: Renew and reawaken. Imbolc is a celebration of renewal, making it the perfect time for a collective fresh start.
    - Big spring cleanup: Dedicate the day to decluttering and purifying your physical spaces. Work together as a coven to clear out old energy by helping each other sort through belongings, clean sacred spaces, and remove what no longer serves you.

Declutter with intention, focusing on items or energies that symbolize stagnation or negativity.

» **Shared garage sale or swap meet:** Plan a shared garage sale for the following weekend to pass on pre-loved items to others who can use them. Alternatively, hold a swap meet among coven members to exchange items and give them new life. This act of sharing reinforces the cycle of renewal and abundance.

» **Bless your spaces:** After cleaning, perform a simple blessing ritual in each space. Light a white candle and pass it through the area, saying, "*From winter's slumber, energy renews - blessed be this space, and all who dwell within.*"

» **Evening of creativity and connection:** Close the day with an intimate gathering. Light candles and invite each coven member to bring a poem, piece of writing, or artwork to share. Sip on wine, mead, or herbal tea while celebrating the creative spirit. This activity honors Brigid as the goddess of poetry, art, and healing, aligning perfectly with the themes of Imbolc.

» **Plant new seeds (literally and figuratively):** As a symbol of new beginnings, each member can plant seeds in small pots. As you plant, set an intention for the coming season - whether it's personal growth, creative ambition, or emotional renewal. Take these home as reminders of your Imbolc intentions.

★ **Additional ideas for Imbolc:**

» **Candle blessing ceremony:** Dedicate white candles to your intentions for the year. Write your goals or desires on the candles, light them, and let their flame carry your wishes into the universe.

» **Craft a Brigid's cross or corn dolly:** Create a Brigid's cross or corn dolly together as a symbol of protection and renewal, placing it on your altar or hanging it in your home.

» **Outdoor connection:** Take a group walk in nature to observe the first signs of life returning. Use this as a meditation on the cycles of renewal and transformation.

OSTARA (SPRING EQUINOX)

- DATE: March 20-23 (northern hemisphere), September 20-23 (southern hemisphere).
- LAND: Day and night stand equal; spring has arrived, plants are flowering, and animals are birthing.
- LIFE: A time to honor the young God and the positive balance between men and women.
- ALTAR ITEMS: Green and yellow candles, eggs.
- RITUAL: Plant your future! Gather together and plan a new flowerbed (either outside or in pots) of sweetly scented buds and herbs. As you sow the seeds, chant a charm for good fortune: "New life we bring forth from the earth: in our hearts, homes, and minds we are blessed by the Divine."
- COVEN ACTIVITY: Celebrate renewal and abundance. Ostara is a joyous celebration of balance and renewal, perfect for rituals and activities that embrace both nature and community.
    - PLANT YOUR FUTURE: Gather as a coven to create a flowerbed, herb garden, or container garden. Choose plants and flowers that are meaningful to your intentions, such as lavender for peace,

basil for abundance, or daisies for joy. As you sow the seeds, chant together: "*New life we bring forth from the earth: in our hearts, homes, and minds we are blessed by the divine.*" Each coven member can also plant seeds in a small pot to take home, nurturing them as a reminder of the intentions set during Ostara.

» Chocolate egg hunt: Host a playful egg hunt using chocolate eggs or decorated hard-boiled eggs. Hide them in a garden or outdoor space and invite coven members to search for them, symbolizing the joy of discovery and the rewards of renewal. To add a magickal touch, inscribe symbols or intentions on the eggs before hiding them.
» Balance ritual: To honor the equinox, perform a ritual that celebrates balance. Create a scale on your altar using two small bowls or plates, one for masculine energy and one for feminine. Have each coven member add an item (such as a flower, crystal, or coin) to each side while stating a quality they wish to balance in their lives, such as compassion and strength, intuition and logic, or action and rest.

★ Outdoor feast of renewal: Host a picnic or outdoor feast featuring fresh spring foods such as leafy greens and seasonal vegetables, and light, floral-infused drinks. This shared meal honors the abundance of nature and the joy of community.
★ Creative expression: Celebrate the season's creative energy with a group art project, such as decorating eggs, painting flowerpots, or creating a shared Ostara mandala using flowers, leaves, and natural items.
★ Additional ideas for Ostara:

» Blessing the land: Take a walk in nature and leave offerings such as birdseed, flower petals, or biodegradable items as a way to honor the earth and its renewal.
» Balance meditation: Practice a group meditation focusing on harmony and equilibrium. Visualize balancing the light and dark within yourselves, reflecting the equinox's energy.
» Egg magick: Use eggs as a focus for a personal or group spell. Write intentions on eggshells and bury them in the earth as a symbol of planting your dreams.

BELTANE

- ★ **Date:** May 1 (northern hemisphere), October 31 (southern hemisphere).
- ★ **Land:** a time of passion and sensuality. In times of old, people made love in the fields to ensure the fertility of the upcoming year's crops.
- ★ **Life:** Honor the fertility of your life.
- ★ **Altar items:** Red and white ribbons and candles.
- ★ **Ritual:** The maypole dance is the traditional celebration of this event. Dress in red and white; burn lavender in a fire and jump over it to ensure the fertility of body, mind, and spirit in the coming year.
- ★ **Coven Activity:** Ignite the fires of creativity and passion. Beltane is a celebration of life in full bloom, making it the perfect time for rituals and activities that honor passion, vitality, and community connection.

    - » **Maypole dance:** If possible, gather outdoors and erect a maypole adorned with long, colorful ribbons. Dance around the pole, weaving the ribbons together as a symbol of unity, creativity, and the intertwining of energies. Each coven member can focus on a personal or group intention while participating in the dance.
    - » **Sacred fire ceremony:** Light a bonfire or a large candle to honor the transformative energy of Beltane. As a group, write down intentions for the coming season on slips of paper. Toss them into the flames as an offering, visualizing your desires manifesting with the fire's power. Jumping over the flames (or a smaller, symbolic flame) can also symbolize purification and a leap into new beginnings.
    - » **Flower crown crafting:** Work together to create flower crowns using seasonal blooms. Wear them during your celebration as a symbol of vitality and connection to nature. This activity also serves as a creative way to honor the Goddess and the earth's abundance.
    - » **Outdoor feast of passion:** Share a feast filled with fresh, vibrant foods such as berries, honey, bread, and seasonal vegetables. Incorporate dishes and drinks infused with warming spices like cinnamon or ginger to reflect the fire of Beltane.

Toast with mead, cider, or herbal tea, and celebrate the bonds of your coven.

- **Union ritual:** Perform a ritual that celebrates the union of energies - masculine and feminine, active and receptive, light and dark. Pair off within the coven or work as a group to symbolically unite these forces, using ribbons, candles, or shared affirmations to represent harmony and creation. If you are a group of consenting adults, now is the time to make love in the fields to ensure the procreative energy of the land moving forward.
- **Night of celebration:** Stay up late to revel in the spirit of Beltane. Dance, sing, drum, or share poetry around the fire. This celebration of joy and passion is a powerful way to honor the vibrant energy of the season.

★ Additional ideas for Beltane:

- **Blessing the land:** Take a walk through nature and leave offerings such as flower petals, seeds, or eco-friendly items to honor the earth's fertility and abundance.
- **Handfasting ceremony:** If anyone in the coven wishes to renew vows or symbolically commit to a new path, Beltane is a perfect time for a handfasting ritual.
- **Sacred connection meditation:** As a group, meditate on the connections between yourselves, the earth, and the divine. Visualize your shared energy blooming like a flower, bringing joy and creativity into all aspects of life.
- **Community outreach:** Use Beltane as an opportunity to spread abundance. Organize a community cleanup or plant trees and flowers as a coven, giving back to the earth in celebration of her gifts.

LITHA (SUMMER SOLSTICE)

- ★ DATE: June 20-23 (northern hemisphere), December 20-23 (southern hemisphere).
- ★ LAND: The longest day of the year with the sun at its peak of power - from this day it will begin the descent to the dark of winter.
- ★ LIFE: Celebrate all that is abundant in life but temper that joy with a solemn respect for endings, for as surely as everything comes, everything also goes.
- ★ ALTAR ITEMS: Sunflowers, cauldron with hot coals inside, and incense of myrrh and frankincense.
- ★ RITUAL: Do a divination by gazing at the patterns formed by the hot coals in your cauldron.
- ★ COVEN ACTIVITY: Embrace the vitality of the sun. Litha, the Summer Solstice, is a celebration of the sun at its peak power. It's a time to honor life, energy, and abundance. Gather your coven for activities that connect you to the vibrant energy of the season and the natural world.
  - » FLORAL CROWN CRAFTING: Begin the day by crafting floral crowns using wildflowers, herbs, and greenery. As you weave the flowers together, focus on intentions of joy, vitality, and growth. Wear the crowns throughout your celebration as a symbol of connection to the earth and the life-giving power of the sun.
  - » SUN WHEEL CREATIONS: Work as a group to create sun wheels from natural materials like vines, branches, and flowers. Decorate them with yellow and gold ribbons to symbolize the sun. Use the wheels as altar decorations or hang them in your home as a reminder of the sun's energy throughout the year.
  - » ENERGIZING MOVEMENT: Celebrate the sun with movement-based activities like outdoor yoga, tai chi, or an energizing dance session. Practice under the noonday sun to fully connect with its warmth and power. Alternatively, form a drumming circle to raise energy and celebrate life's rhythm, inviting participants to drum, dance, and sing together.
  - » SOLSTICE FIRE CEREMONY: As the sun begins to set, gather around a bonfire or large candle to honor the day's energy. Write

down intentions or affirmations on small pieces of paper and toss them into the fire, visualizing them being carried to the heavens by the flames. Share stories, songs, or poetry that celebrate life and light.

» **Solar meditation:** Practice a guided meditation as a group, focusing on the sun's energy infusing your body with vitality and strength. Visualize the light filling you with warmth, radiance, and the power to manifest your intentions.
» **Outdoor feast:** Share a solstice-inspired feast featuring fresh, vibrant foods like fruits, salads, and herbal teas. Include solar-themed treats, such as lemon cakes or sun-shaped bread. Toast with sparkling drinks or infused waters, offering gratitude for the abundance of the season.
» **Blessing of the waters:** If you have access to a natural body of water, such as a river, lake, or ocean, perform a water blessing ceremony. Use flower petals or biodegradable offerings to honor the sacred balance between the sun's fire and the water's cool, healing energy.

★ **Additional ideas for Litha:**

» **Sunrise greeting:** Begin your celebration by watching the sunrise together, honoring the light's longest journey across the sky. Meditate or set intentions for the day ahead.
» **Solar crafts:** Make candles infused with herbs and oils that symbolize the sun, such as calendula, chamomile, or orange. Use them in future rituals as a reminder of Litha's energy.
» **Community giving:** Use the energy of the solstice to give back. Organize a community cleanup or plant sunflowers as a group to honor the earth and the sun's power.
» **Circle of gratitude:** End the day by forming a circle and sharing something each coven member is grateful for, celebrating the abundance of life and community.

LAMMAS

- **Date:** August 1 (northern hemisphere), February 1 (southern hemisphere).
- **Land:** The first harvest; food is put away for winter. The days are still long and hot, but the dark is approaching. The traditional food to eat at this time is bread and corn.
- **Life:** A time to honor the rewards of hard labor and the results of plans and goals made in the previous year that have come to fruition.

- **Altar items:** Corn, dried plants, and fruits.
- **Ritual:** Bury any attitudes or habits that no longer serve you by writing them down, wrapping them around a stone, and burying them deep in the earth.
- **Coven activity:** Harvesting gratitude and transformation. Lammas celebrates the harvest, both literal and metaphorical, making it the perfect time for activities that focus on gratitude, abundance, and letting go of what no longer serves.
    - **Bread-baking ritual:** Gather as a coven to bake bread together, symbolizing the fruits of your labor. Choose recipes that reflect the season, such as a rustic loaf, cornbread, or herb-infused rolls. As you knead the dough, focus on your gratitude for the abundance in your life, infusing it with positive energy. Before baking, inscribe symbols of prosperity or gratitude into the dough. Share the bread as a sacred meal during your gathering, affirming that the positive application of body, will, and spirit brings desired results.
    - **Harvest gratitude circle:** Sit in a circle and share what each member is grateful for, reflecting on the achievements, lessons, and blessings of the past year. Pass a basket of dried corn or wheat around, and as each person speaks, they can add a small token of

gratitude (such as a flower petal, herb, or seed) to the basket. This creates a shared symbol of your collective abundance.

- **Creative harvest offering:** Each coven member can create an offering that symbolizes their personal harvest - a small bundle of herbs, a piece of fruit, or a handwritten note of gratitude. Place these offerings on the altar or bury them in the earth as a way to honor the cycle of giving and receiving.
- **Releasing ritual:** During the ritual, write down habits, attitudes, or patterns you wish to release. Wrap them around a small stone, symbolizing their weight, and bury the stone in the earth. As you bury it, visualize the earth absorbing and transforming the energy, making space for new growth and possibilities.
- **Seasonal feast:** Share a meal that celebrates the harvest, featuring foods such as freshly baked bread, seasonal fruits and vegetables, and dishes infused with grains. Decorate the table with corn husks, dried flowers, and candles to create a festive and sacred atmosphere.
- **Seasonal crafting:** Work together to craft corn dollies, wheat bundles, or small charms from natural materials. These can serve as symbols of protection and abundance for the coming months, or as offerings for your altar.

★ **Additional ideas for Lammas:**

- **Outdoor gratitude walk:** Take a walk in nature, observing the abundance of the season. Leave small offerings like flower petals, birdseed, or biodegradable items as thanks to the land for its gifts.
- **Coven vision board:** Collaborate on a shared vision board, reflecting on what you wish to bring into the next cycle. Use images, words, and symbols that represent your collective intentions.
- **Firelight reflection:** End the evening around a small fire or a candle circle. Reflect on the duality of abundance and release, symbolized by the light of the flame and the encroaching darkness.

HOW TO MAKE A CORN DOLLY FOR LAMMAS

- Gather dried corn husks (or long stalks of wheat, oat, or barley if available). Soak them briefly in warm water to make them pliable.
- Choose three to five husks and tie them together near the top with natural twine or string - this forms the head.
- Fold the husks downward over the tie and shape into a body. Wrap string beneath the head to define the neck.
- Separate husks into arms (optional), and tie off at the ends. You can braid, wrap, or leave loose.
- Shape a skirt or legs, depending on your design. If you're creating a skirt, gather and tie the husks around the waist to hold the shape, then trim the ends for symmetry. If making legs, divide the husks in two, shape and tie each individually.
- Allow it to dry fully, and then bless your corn dolly with a simple charm:

Spirit of grain, of sun and seed,
Bless this home [or our lives] with all we need.

- Place it on your coven altar to honor the harvest spirit and carry your coven intentions through the turning of the year.

MABON (AUTUMN EQUINOX)

- ★ **Date:** September 20-23 (northern hemisphere), March 20-23 (southern hemisphere).
- ★ **Land:** Day and night stand equal as the second harvest is stored.
- ★ **Life:** A time to reflect on the coming rest and respite of winter.
- ★ **Altar items:** Autumn leaves, brown and orange candles, dried flowers, wood, and bracken.
- ★ **Ritual:** Meditate on death by lying together on the ground in "dead pose" (flat on back with hands down to the side), radiating out in a circle with heads touching.
- ★ **Coven activity:** Reflecting on balance and gratitude. Mabon celebrates the balance of light and dark, making it the perfect time for activities that honor reflection, connection, and gratitude for the abundance of the year.
    - » **Sunset reflection ritual:** Gather your coven in a natural setting to watch the sunset together. Before the sun dips below the horizon, take turns sharing something you are grateful for and something you are ready to release. This moment of reflection symbolizes the balance of Mabon and the transition into the quieter months.
    - » **Meditation on death and renewal:** Lie on the ground together in the "dead pose," radiating out in a circle with your heads touching. Meditate on the cycle of life, death, and rebirth, visualizing yourself releasing old energy into the earth. Imagine the earth transforming this energy, preparing you for renewal in the months ahead. End the meditation by sitting up and taking a collective deep breath, symbolizing the transition from stillness to renewed vitality.
    - » **Harvest gratitude altar:** As a group, create an altar using autumn leaves, apples, dried flowers, and other seasonal items. Invite each coven member to place a token of gratitude on the altar, such as a written note, a small charm, or a harvest item like a piece

of fruit. Reflect on the abundance of the season and the intentions for the darker months ahead.

- » **Seasonal feast and sharing:** Share a potluck-style meal featuring hearty, seasonal dishes like roasted vegetables, soups, breads, and apple-based desserts. Incorporate symbolic foods like pomegranates, pears, and nuts to honor the second harvest. Use this time to connect, share stories, and celebrate the community you've built.
- » **Balance and gratitude circle:** Form a circle and pass around a small balance scale. Each coven member can add a token (like a stone or flower) to one side, representing what they are releasing, and to the other side, representing what they are grateful for. This simple yet powerful ritual visually reinforces the balance and gratitude of Mabon.
- » **Crafting and connection:** Work together to create seasonal crafts such as autumn wreaths, herbal sachets, or nature-based charms. These can be taken home or used as offerings to honor the season.

★ **Additional ideas for Mabon:**

- » **Candlelit labyrinth walk:** Create a simple labyrinth with candles or stones and take turns walking through it. As you walk, reflect on your journey through the year, ending with gratitude for the harvest and preparation for winter.
- » **Nature gratitude walk:** Take a walk together in a wooded area or park, collecting fallen leaves or natural items. Leave small biodegradable offerings as thanks to the land for its abundance.
- » **Bonfire of reflection:** If safe and feasible, light a bonfire to represent the balance of light and dark. Write down things you wish to release and toss them into the fire, visualizing transformation and renewal.

FINAL THOUGHTS

I encourage you to create and personalize your own celebrations of the Sabbats whenever possible. Witchcraft is not about following rigid scripts or adhering to someone else's idea of what is "correct" or "approved" - not even mine!

Your unique perspective, creativity, and connection to the earth are essential ingredients in crafting truly honoring and empowered rituals.

It is important to really make an effort to meet for the Sabbats, at the very least the four greater ones. However, sometimes it's just not possible. On those occasions, a shared ritual or dedication - spoken simultaneously, wherever each member is - can still be profoundly powerful. Intention knows no bounds.

In closing this chapter, I want to encourage you all to be bold and spontaneous in your work together as a coven. Try not to be worried about doing things wrong when working magick as a group.

Remember . . .

- ★ There are no mistakes in witchcraft, only lessons.
- ★ Obstacles are opportunities for positive change and growth.
- ★ Be patient and persevere: anything worthwhile takes effort.
- ★ Experiment, explore, and enjoy!

CHAPTER 11

MAGICKAL GATHERINGS

Magickal gatherings don't necessarily have to be intense coven gatherings of Wiccan initiates to raise power. Events like goddess gatherings are a great way to mix socializing and magick and to let non-Wiccan friends share our enchanted lifestyles! A goddess gathering is pretty much a dinner party for goddesses only, with a ritual and some spellcasting thrown in.

Anyone can attend: the only prerequisite is an open heart and an open mind. It's lovely, because people who are not sure about being full-blown witches can experience some magick-making in a safe and fun environment.

Remember: It is your comprehension of the world around you that allows it to manifest and speak to you in an enchanted way. Look for magick and it will make itself known to you.

GODDESS GATHERINGS

My first goddess gathering came about when my good girlfriend Coral and I were chatting one afternoon. She is a brilliant garden designer with an amazing appreciation of beauty in nature, and is very in tune with the earth, the seasons, and the phases of the moon. We were discussing how a full moon was coming up in a couple of weeks, and that it happened to fall on the witches' sacred Sabbat of Mabon - the Autumn Equinox, when day and night stand equal.

We both agreed it would be nice to have a girls-only dinner party under the full moon at Coral's home in the Topanga Canyon above Malibu. The plan was for the (mortal!) goddesses to arrive at 8 pm, conduct the ritual at 8.30 pm, and then eat, drink, and be merry until the witching hour!

The first step was to invite the goddesses. Most of Coral's friends didn't know much about witchcraft but were open to new experiences and loved the exotic sound of a gathering. I also needed to create an outline for the ritual we would be doing, so we could let everyone know what they needed to bring. I decided to keep it fairly simple, with the main focus being transformation and having great desires realized.

This is the email we sent out:

> Goddesses!
>
> It is time to gather under a full moon
>
> To bewitch and share good cheer.
>
> A night of empowerment and enchantment awaits
>
> Be at Coral's at the stroke of eight!
>
> Our full moon magick starts at 8.30 pm with a spellbinding supper afterwards. Come dressed opulently in lush pinks and reds, like the luscious goddesses you are! Bring with you on a piece of paper a list of your deepest desires – for this is the night that your dreams come true!

The next step was to create an appropriate menu. Our gathering was happening at Mabon - a festival of the harvest when food would be stored away for the coming cold and dark of winter. In the world of magick, it is a time to acknowledge the rewards of our hard labor and rest secure in the knowledge that the universe always provides if we accept it. Partnered with the conjuring power of a full moon, our menu needed to feature foods of the harvest: dried fruits, nuts, root vegetables, and grains. We also needed food and beverages to honor the Goddess: apples for love and berries for abundance, and sweet mead, fine champagne, and sparkling grape juice (for the non-drinkers like me!) as libations to her.

Here is our menu for that Mabon feast - feel free to use it, or be inspired to create something that works with what you can access and enjoy.

FULL MOON MABON GODDESS GATHERING MENU

Everything on this menu is created with magick in mind!

APPETIZER

- Dried fruits and nuts - symbolic of the successful harvest as experienced on the land and in our lives.
- Brie and strawberries - passionate and romantic, these foods are sacred to love.

MAIN

- Moroccan vegetable stew with couscous/ brown rice - this rich and hearty stew celebrates the harvest and blesses our endeavors.
- Breads - sacred to the harvest - remind us that trusting in our dreams and desires and honoring our efforts and experiences guarantees a unique and richly rewarding life.

DESSERT

- Blackberry and apple tart - berries are the fruits of passion and apples are sacred to Aphrodite.

LIBATIONS

- Moët & Chandon champagne.
- Sparkling grape juice for abundance.
- Honey mead to toast the moon during our ritual.

When you are planning the menu, research the magickal meanings of foods using books and the internet, but don't be afraid to use your intuition and imagination too. For example, if berries are in season and looking lush, ripe, and sweet, and you have decided your ritual will be for fertility, then they will be perfect as they obviously evoke an appreciation of the qualities of fertility.

On the night of the gathering

That night, I arrived early at Coral's and she had already made everything look lovely. The dining table was outside and decorated with white and pink flowers, fairy lights, and shimmering glitter; overhead, hanging from a tree was a candelabra lit with tiny scented candles.

A little distance away behind some trees was a circular stone table and benches. I set about transforming the setting from a picnic area into a mystical grove. I put symbols of the four elements on the table and in the center I placed a large cast iron cauldron and an altar candle. I set out 12 glasses (we would be toasting the moon and pouring libations to the Goddess) and alongside these placed 12 little red rose-scented candles for love. Next to the cauldron, I set a vase in which were 12 long-stemmed roses. Then I scattered tea light candles in glass jars in the surrounding plants and trees. The whole area looked like a fairy grove, potent and ready to make magick in.

By this time the goddesses had started to arrive. Everyone was laughing and smiling and looking divine. The dress code of opulent and goddess-like was definitely honored!

When everyone was assembled, I gave a little speech about what we would be doing: a ritual to honor our efforts over the past year, and then we would invoke our new dreams into reality.

We gathered in a circle around the table, eyes bright and full of expectancy. First, I talked through the details of what we would be doing. It's important to familiarize everyone with the general outline so you can all relax and focus on the feeling of being in the space without worrying about having to remember things and what comes next.

Full moon goddess gathering ritual

I started by chanting my favorite Sanskrit chant. It is used in the track called "AM" on my solo album *Witch Web* - streaming on Spotify and other streaming services. It is very euphoric and always unites everyone's energy psychically and emotionally. Then I sprinkled some incense on the burning discs, and as the air filled with an entrancing scent, I cast a circle by formally acknowledging our sacred space and invoking the elements.

Then it came time to declare the Goddess present in circle as a part of the circle-casting ritual. I asked everyone, in turn, to take a rose from the vase and pass it to the woman to her left, bestowing a kiss on each cheek and saying, "[*Name*], *thou art goddess.*" Although some of us were strangers, in this moment we were all intimate, united as goddesses. A warm feeling of love and acceptance filled our circle so strongly that it brought tears to my eyes.

We then joined hands as I declared:

Tonight we sisters gather, under a full and harvest moon
On this sacred night of the Equinox.
We honor what we have and what we yet have not;
We celebrate our challenges and rewards of successful schemes;
And on the wings of magick, we fly toward our dreams.

Then, one at a time, we each lit our little red love candle from the large altar candle flame and then read our wishes out loud. As accompaniment, at first I alone sang the "Wiccan Goddess Chant" - *"Isis, Astarte, Diana, Hecate, Demeter, Kali, Inanna"* - but it didn't take long before the other goddesses joined in. When her list was read, each goddess threw it into the cauldron with a sprinkled pinch of incense, fanning the spirals of smoke to the sky, carrying her wishes with it.

After the final list was read, we all joined hands and really started chanting to raise power. As our voices grew in intensity, tingles went up my spine and I could tangibly feel our cone of power extending into the heavens. All the animals around us could sense it too, because all of a sudden dogs started howling, birds started calling, and crickets chirping. All of nature was joining us in intent and desire. It was truly amazing! At the peak of the cone, we ceased together intuitively and I called out:

By one our spell is done,
By two it shall come true,
By three so mote it be,
By four for the good of all,
By five our dreams come alive.

Then we all clapped our hands once in unison and quickly rested them on the ground to let the energy drain out.

We each raised a glass of mead to toast - "to the goddess, to us!" - and then poured a little on the ground as libations to her and to ourselves.

Then it was time for our feast. Our dinner conversation was not the usual fare - it was deep and thoughtful, hilarious and revealing. United we drew strength from each other's sharing of experiences, triumphs, and tragedies.

As the evening finally drew to a close, I reminded the goddesses not to speak of what had transpired on this night: spells that are cast are best served with silent respect, trusting them to whisk away and do their business. Gossiping and constant going over the events would be like planting a seed and then digging it up to see how it's going.

We left the gathering changed - reinvigorated and renewed.

Well, I'm sure you're dying to know . . . did the spells work? I can tell you mine certainly did! I needed a shift and some clarity in a situation relating to someone who seemed to care for me but was constantly sending mixed signals. Within a day of doing the spell, all of a sudden that person was very clear with their intentions. The shift in their attitude was so remarkable I could only put it down to the spell.

The other goddesses all experienced results, ranging from job promotions, to love restored, to being confronted with the very difficulties they sought to avoid (but instead of being thwarted by them, they had the energy to blast through the problem and resolve the issue that was blocking them from happiness).

The wonderful thing about creating something like a goddess gathering is not just the results of the spells cast. You realize that, when joined with others in a magickal mindset, your whole life is a work of magick, an expression of your unique creative essence.

The more goddess gatherings and other magickal moments you create in your life; the more wonderful life becomes.

Goddess gathering checklist

Here is a checklist to help you plan your own gathering.

1. Decide on an auspicious date.
2. Write an appropriately charmed invitation.
3. Email or post it out to fellow goddesses.
4. Plan the ritual. Do some research and write up the intent, the process, and the incantations. Decide what contribution each individual goddess should make.
5. Decide what props are needed for the ritual and organize their availability. For example, candles, feathers, flowers, shells, incense, cauldron, etc.
6. Plan the magickal menu. Again do research and choose foods that relate to your magickal event and goals. And while you are deciding on food, you may like to also decide on the music that will add an extra dimension to the evening's entrancement.
7. Once the RSVPs start flooding in, send out another email informing each goddess of what she will personally need to provide for the gathering. For example, her wish list for the spell, an object she would like blessed, etc.
8. Get shopping and cooking. Do as much cooking as you can in advance of the day. You need to be feeling relaxed and ready to make magick too on the night, not absolutely trashed from a hell day in the kitchen!
9. Perhaps plan a gift for each of the goddesses. After our gathering, everyone left with the rose they were given and the candle they lit.
10. Type up the goddess menu and a clear outline of the ritual in large bold print that you can keep on hand to help guide you throughout the proceedings. Having said this, though,

it's important that you try to memorize everything, so the proceedings can go smoothly and to maximum magickal effect.

11. The day before, rehearse your ritual and memorize the words you need to.
12. On the day, relax and go with the flow; let spontaneous things happen, but as much as possible stick to the planned ritual so that the power raised is focused for good and maximum effect.
13. Delegate any chores you can so that you don't have so much on your plate that you can't be a goddess on the night!

A tip: The trick to guaranteeing a special and successful ritual is careful planning and practice. This means running through the proceedings in your mind before the event and learning all the invocations and incantations off by heart. When you are actually doing the ritual, people can repeat after the person who leads, but at least one person needs to be very familiar with what is going on.

Another tip: It is better that no one drinks too much before the ritual. One glass of wine perhaps is fine, but if everyone is sloshed there will be more giggling than granting of wishes.

Good occasions for a goddess gathering

Full moons and new moons are always a good excuse, as are solstices, equinoxes, and Sabbats. Also, gatherings don't only have to be at night: dawn, midday, sunset, and twilight are all special, evocative, and atmospheric times.

Birthdays, anniversaries, and other events such as these are generally not a good idea as they focus too much on an individual and not enough on the collective. The key to a successful goddess gathering where both magick and merriment are invoked is a unified purpose and egoless state in each individual.

GOD GATHERINGS

Of course you can host a god gathering! The same general principles apply: create a sacred space, align your intentions, and celebrate the divine masculine in all its forms.

A FEW TIPS FOR A MEANINGFUL GATHERING

- Honor the masculine energy: Explore the archetypes of the divine masculine - protector, nurturer, creator, and innovator. Incorporate rituals or activities that celebrate strength, wisdom, and balance, such as storytelling, drumming, or crafting.
- Sacred shared responsibility: Keep the energy harmonious by sharing responsibilities for cooking, cleaning, and preparation. A god gathering is a chance to embody the spirit of collaboration and mutual respect.
- Themes and symbols: Work with symbols of the God, such as the sun, stag, oak tree, or serpent, depending on the deity you're honoring. Rituals can focus on transformation, action, or grounding - qualities often associated with masculine energies.
- Have fun: While the gathering can be spiritual, it doesn't have to be overly serious. Share laughter, good food, and camaraderie. Games, challenges, or even a fire-building contest can reflect the active, dynamic qualities of the God.

A god gathering, like any magickal gathering, is about balance, connection, and honoring the sacred energy within and around you. Make it a celebration of both joy and purpose.

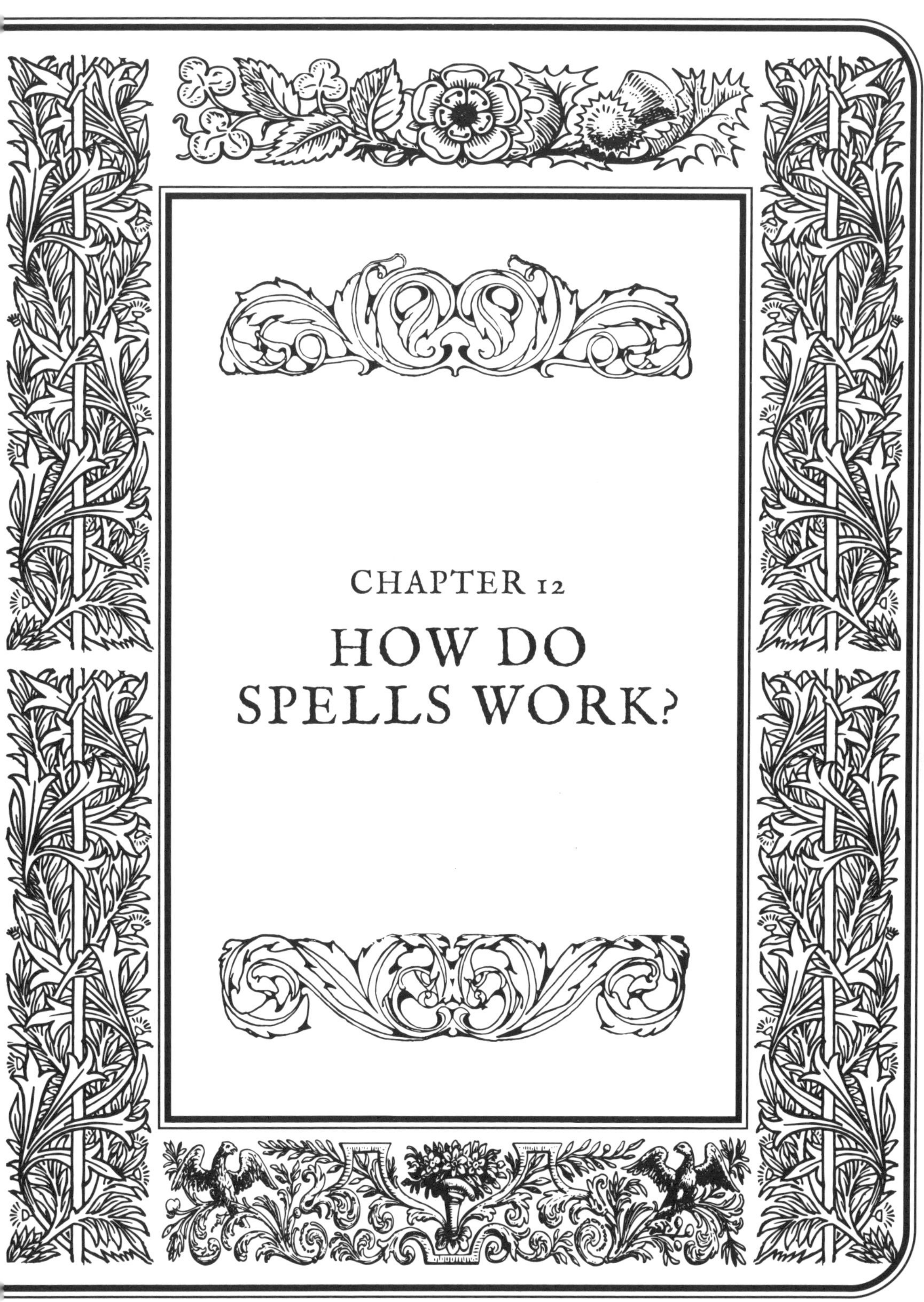

CHAPTER 12

HOW DO SPELLS WORK?

Part of an eclectic coven's work is to create their own "tradition" and research, collate, and most importantly create the rituals and spells that will form their practice. But sometimes it is good to have a few tried and true rituals or spells to get you going.

There are now many books out there which can help, including my spell book *Lost Book of Spells*, which includes over 150 spells and rituals bridging ancient wisdom and our modern world. But how can you be sure a spell will work?

This is something I have spent a lot of time thinking about. I am not an irrational or illogical person and I have analyzed the processes that I think creates the often-extraordinary results experienced - and it is that people need to find the key that unlocks their individual belief that something extraordinary is possible. Not everyone who goes to a Tony Robbins seminar becomes a multi-millionaire, but some do. In the same way, not every spell works, but many do. Science acknowledges that part of the world manifesting the way it does is because of the way we perceive it. We need to believe something extraordinary is possible in order to switch on the potential for what we want to manifest.

That's why spells can work - because often the concept of them and the process of them stimulates something deep inside us. It triggers hope and awakens the child within who once lived in a world full of enchantment and magick and infinite possibilities.

These days, I do a lot more rituals than spells, and there is a difference. A ritual is like building a home, and spells are the furniture you put in it. In my craft, I concentrate on building a strong home that people can visit safely, and with maximum enjoyment, if they choose.

Maybe this has to do with my lengthy years of practicing - it is appropriate now that I spend more time in service to others. But to do this the best I can, I have to be spiritually strong, and that's where rituals and observances are aligned.

Spellcasting is a powerful activity but there is also a power in the symbols, words, herbs, crystals, colors, numbers, and phases of the moon. That power manifests when we recognize it too. If we look to it, it makes itself visible.

As the Western world continues to awaken to (and remember) the subtle energies of existence, psychic powers, kinetic powers, all those "super" natural qualities that we have, so they will awaken and evolve within us, becoming more present, more relevant, and more powerful.

As a species, we must continue to evolve: death, destruction, pain, and suffering are all necessary in the cycles of life. But when these dark experiences are tempered with acceptance, honor, and respect, they cease to rule us and instead become our trials of strength that we can face and embrace bravely, and even with gratitude, for they hold us together and give us a point of reference to encourage us to keep moving forward. Then we can know that love, goodness, and compassion manifesting as growth and enlightenment are the

foundations upon which we build our lives and are the most powerful expressions of our existence in this extraordinary universe.

Your world will be as magickal as you let it be; as soon as you start doubting what you are doing and feeling that it is silly or rubbish, then it will be.

A very simple analogy I like to use to explain this is: imagine you are at a dinner party, sitting at a table with 12 other people and everyone is speaking Italian. You don't speak Italian. You listen to the babble around you and watch the wild gestures and expressive movements of the people passionately talking and it all seems fun, but baffling! You have barely any idea of what is going on. However, if you learn the language suddenly a fascinating world appears, full of interesting stories, passion and excitement and, most importantly, understanding and communion.

It is the same for awakening your witchiness. Learn the language of magick and the world becomes a magickal place! That seemingly elusive, ethereal otherworld of real magick can be a lot closer than you think - it is inside you, in your desires, hopes, fears, and dreams. Open the door to that world inside you and watch the world around you shift and change and shape itself to be everything you dreamed it could be, and a lot more!

THE TIPPING POINT

Here's a selection of general tips and ideas that may equip you to see obstacles as opportunities and trials as transformation.

Stick with it

The beauty of practicing the craft both as a solitary and as part of a coven is that the experience becomes more textured, complex, and deeper yet easier as you go along. Persevere through the teething stage. What was once an effort to remember and organize shifts to become intuitive. You learn to "trust your gut," thus conjuring

satisfying spiritual and magickal experiences effortlessly. It's as if you awaken an age-old sense of what it is to be human, aligned with the grace and wonder of this universe - when the stress of our modern lives can often have us feeling in battle with it. Know that not even the smallest magickal act is wasted; they all contribute to the divine tapestry of life that we co-create.

I did it my way

Don't feel you have to abide by someone else's way of doing things as if they're standing over your shoulder judging you. You will never feel and experience real, tangible magick if you seek it solely outside yourself. Learn to cultivate it within you, and trust how this feels.

Just chill

The more complicated and elaborate a ritual is doesn't necessarily mean it is more powerful. Be relaxed, confident, and deeply connected emotionally, spiritually, and physically with your intent. Then it will be more powerful and effective to simply light a red candle and make a wish for love than spend a whole day concocting an elaborate ritual only to perform it feeling un-centered and distracted by worrying about getting it right. Magickal transformation occurs outside the physical construct of linear time, and you can indeed trust that you are experiencing infinite potential the moment a shiver goes up your spine, or you feel "different" as the spell is cast or the ritual evoked.

Believe in yourself - trust your inner voice, trust your methods, trust your choices. You are witch, and that is enough. The magick has started.

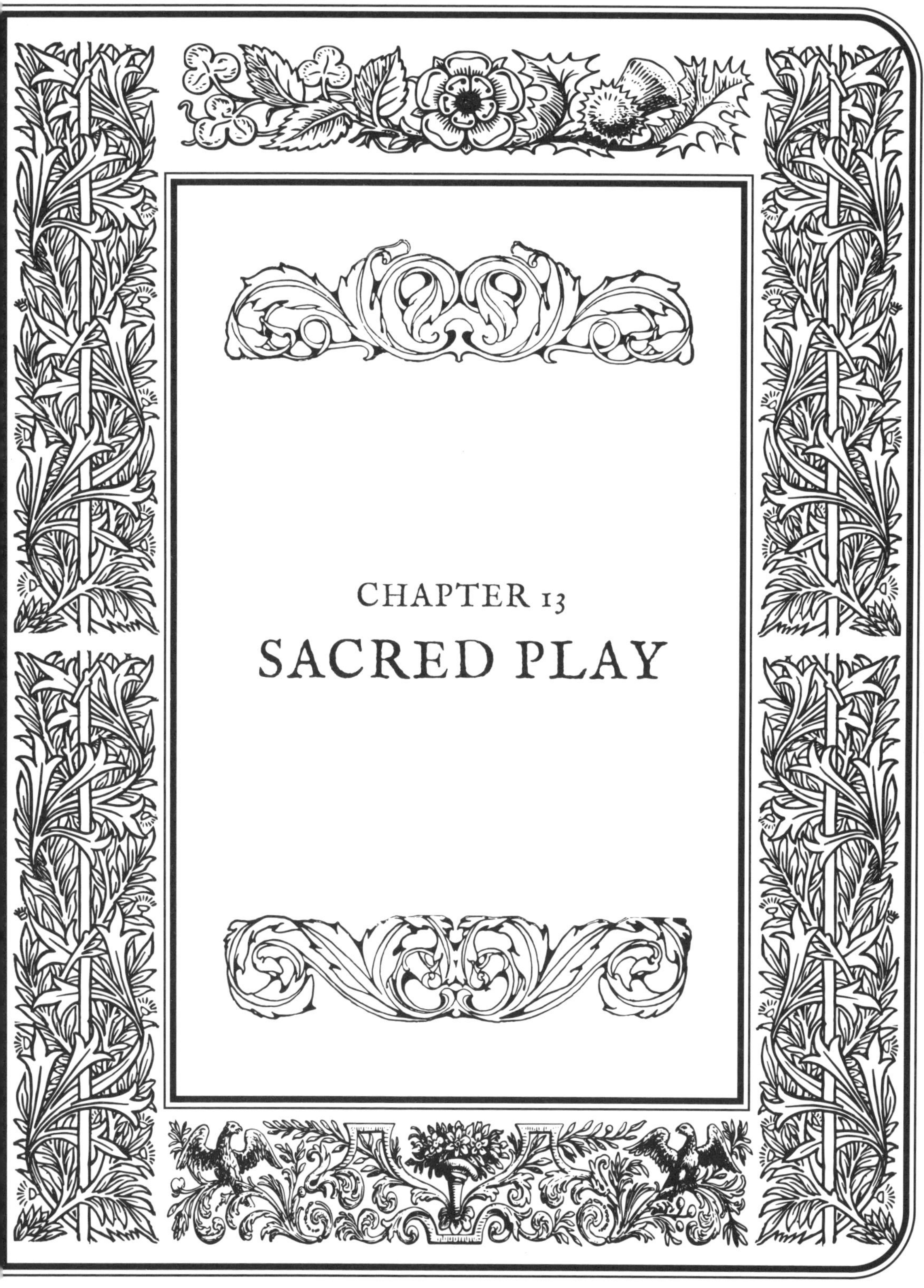

CHAPTER 13

SACRED PLAY

As you and your coven deepen your connection and refine your craft, you might feel inspired to unwind and share some lighthearted, joyful experiences together, outside of your dedicated coven work. There are countless fun and enriching activities you can enjoy together, strengthening your bond in both the physical world and your shared covenworld. Let the magick flow and the laughter follow!

SHOPPING WITH A MAGICKAL TWIST

Why not skip the usual mall crawl and plan a day of magickal shopping instead? Make it a purposeful outing to enrich your witchy practices and build connections with your coven (or solo spiritual journey).

Start by visiting a metaphysical supply store to stock up on herbs, incense, candles, talismans, and ethically sourced crystals. These treasures will enhance your rituals and spellwork. If your coven has a collective symbol, consider finding matching rings, pendants, or bracelets to wear as a sign of unity and shared intention.

Next, explore a boutique that carries flowing, magickal clothing. If you're feeling creative, browse fabric and craft stores to design your own magickal wear.

Take a break for lunch at a vegetarian, vegan, or organic café. Sharing a meal rooted in nourishment and intention is a beautiful way to bond and recharge.

Finally, spend the afternoon at an esoteric or independent bookstore. Browse the shelves for books on magick, spirituality, astrology, or any topic that calls to you. Whether it's a classic title or a fresh take on the craft, find something that inspires and empowers you.

Turn your shopping day into an intentional journey - one that deepens your connection to the craft and to those who share it with you.

COVEN READING CIRCLES

Reading remains a timeless way to spark imagination, deepen understanding, and create shared experiences - perfect for coven gatherings. A reading circle allows you to connect weekly, diving into a story that resonates with your spiritual and magickal path.

Choosing a work of fantasy or fiction with magickal themes can be an inspired choice as it aligns your collective imagination and enhances group visualizations and meditations. Here are some modern recommendations to enrich your reading circle:

- ★ *The Priory of the Orange Tree* BY SAMANTHA SHANNON: A lush, feminist epic fantasy featuring dragons, forbidden magick, and an intricate web of female-led narratives.
- ★ *A Discovery of Witches* BY DEBORAH HARKNESS: A spellbinding blend of history, romance, and magick, following a witch and a vampire as they uncover ancient secrets.
- ★ *Circe* BY MADELINE MILLER: A stunning retelling of the myth of Circe, weaving themes of power, transformation, and the divine feminine. (A personal favorite of mine!)
- ★ *The Bear and the Nightingale* BY KATHERINE ARDEN: A mesmerizing tale inspired by Russian folklore, filled with wintery enchantment and ancient spirits.

For younger or YA readers, consider:

- *Witches Steeped in Gold* BY CIANNON SMART: A vibrant Caribbean-inspired fantasy about rival witches grappling with destiny and power.
- *The Raven Cycle* BY MAGGIE STIEFVATER: A beautifully atmospheric series blending modern-day mysticism, ley lines, and friendships forged through magick.
- AND MY OWN OFFERING, *Witch: a Summerland Mystery*: What happens when an Australian girl with secret powers moves to California and falls for the hottest guy in school, who happens to have a secret of his own?

Creating a magickal atmosphere

Transform your space into an enchanting retreat for your reading circle. Scatter soft rugs and cushions, light incense, and adorn the room with glowing candles or fairy lights. Bring snacks or herbal tea to share as you immerse yourselves in the story.

Encourage discussion and reflection after reading each chapter or section. How does the book inspire your magickal practice? What imagery, ideas, or themes can you bring into your rituals or meditations?

Beyond the circle

If reading fiction isn't your group's style, consider exploring spiritual or magickal nonfiction together, in addition to my own offerings. There are so many choices - simply choose a subject that expands on your immediate knowledge.

A coven reading circle is more than just a way to enjoy stories - it's a practice of shared discovery, inspiration, and connection, weaving your imaginations into your magickal work.

ORACLES AND TEA-LEAF READING CIRCLES

While tarot often calls for dedicated study and structured interpretation, oracle cards offer a more open and accessible way to explore intuition as a group. Drawing cards together, sharing impressions, meditating on messages, and weaving collective insights can be a beautiful coven activity - both uplifting and enriching. Oracle work invites each member to express their unique spiritual language while strengthening the group's shared connection. Pair this with tea-leaf reading and you create a truly playful and powerful ritual.

WITCHY MOVIE NIGHTS

This is always a favorite! Plan a night (or even an all-day marathon) to enjoy your favorite witchy movies and TV shows. Here's how to make it magickal and modern, while keeping some retro classics in the mix.

Movie recommendations

For my witchy movie nights I always revisit some classics:

- *The Wicker Man* (1973) for its eerie exploration of pagan themes.
- *Bell, Book and Candle* (1958) for a dose of retro romance and glamour.
- *The Witches of Eastwick* (1987), an iconic, deliciously dark classic where Cher, Susan Sarandon, and Michelle Pfeiffer conjure up feminine power, rebellion, and wicked delight in the face of patriarchal charm.

For a modern twist, consider:

- ★ *Practical Magic* 1 (1998) and 2 (due September 2026) are staples for their heartwarming and empowering themes of sisterhood and magick.
- ★ *The Love Witch* (2016), a visually stunning homage to 1960s technicolor witchcraft, dripping with campy charm.
- ★ *Coven* (2020), a hauntingly beautiful tale of sisterhood and resistance during the Basque witch trials.

TV show recommendations

A witchy TV series marathon is another great way to connect. Dust off the classics or dive into something new:

- ★ The original *Buffy the Vampire Slayer* (1997-2003) for timeless battles of good versus evil - and Willow's journey of magick and self-discovery.
- ★ *Charmed* (1998-2006), or its 2018 reboot, for magickal sibling dynamics and spellcasting inspiration.
- ★ *The Chilling Adventures of Sabrina* (2018-2020), for a darker take on the teenage witch narrative.
- ★ *A Discovery of Witches* (2018-2022), blending witchcraft with history, romance, and adventure.
- ★ *Good Witch* (2015-2021), a lighter, feel-good series about magickal intuition and community.
- ★ *Luna Nera* (2020), an Italian historical drama about persecuted women discovering their witch lineage and rising in their power.
- ★ *Siempre Bruja / Always a Witch* (2019-2020), a Colombian series where a time-traveling witch explores love, freedom, and fire magick across centuries.
- ★ *Twin Peaks* (1990-1991) by David Lynch for surreal, dark, and mystical vibes that are as enigmatic as they are inspiring.
- ★ *Witch Hunt* (2020), a Norwegian supernatural thriller where modern-day women are hunted as witches in a society filled with secrets and fear.

Snacks and atmosphere

Make it a cozy and enchanting experience. Scatter cushions and blankets, light a few candles, and brew a pot of herbal tea. For snacks, opt for dried fruit, nuts, popcorn dusted with cinnamon, or dark chocolate. Sparkling fruit juices or herbal-infused waters are perfect witchy drinks.

WORKSHOPS, CLASSES, AND COLLECTIVE LEARNING

One of the most nourishing ways a coven can grow is by learning together. Whether it's through weekend intensives, day-long workshops, or online conferences, educational experiences create a shared language and deepen both skill and community.

These days, the opportunities are limitless. Unlike when I began - when you had to wait for a rare event in your city or scrape together travel costs - modern witches have access to an abundance of global teachings online. From beginner courses in candle magick to deep dives into ancestral healing, astrology, divination, and more, there's something for every path.

One of my favorite examples is WitchCon (witchcon.com), a powerful international online conference. It's an amazing way to connect with magickal minds across the world, from the comfort of your own sacred space.

Encourage your coven to explore options together - attend the same course and set regular catch-ups to discuss what you've learned and how you can apply it to your shared practice. Make it a ritual in itself.

RITUAL OF CHOICE

When the options feel endless, try this simple coven spell to help the right path reveal itself.

You'll need:

- A small flat dish or surface (like a wooden tray)
- A circle of fine sea salt
- A pendulum or crystal point
- A clear line traced across the salt circle, marking one half as yes and the other as no
- Names of the course options written on slips of paper or represented by crystals

To begin:

- Cast a simple circle around the space.
- Place the slips or crystals representing your options along the yes/no line.
- One by one, say the name of the course aloud, hold the pendulum over the line, and ask, "*Is this the path for us?*"
- Allow the pendulum to swing toward yes or no.
- Repeat until one course receives a clear yes from the energy of the group.

Trust what the magick reveals. The course chosen becomes not just a class, but a guided path your coven walks together.

And while online offerings like WitchCon provide incredible access to international teachers and inspiration, there's also something deeply grounding about showing up together in the same physical space. If your coven is ready to take your learning offline, look into workshops, festivals, or retreats happening in your area. You might find weekend intensives on astrology, herbal magick, sigil crafting, or ancestral work - often hosted in private studios, community spaces, or at seasonal gatherings. Attending these events as a coven deepens your bond through shared experience and gives you a fresh spark of insight to bring back into your own circle.

KNITTING AND CROCHETING CIRCLE

Knitting and crocheting are aligned with a powerful type of magick you may read about in various books on the craft called "cord magick." As cords are woven and knotted together, intent and will is sealed and enchanted in the cords. Knitting/crocheting can work the same way. Each member of your coven can knit/crochet squares while chanting affirmations so that each square is empowered. Sew these together and use it as a coven blanket to meditate together under (just lie down and cover yourselves with it), or you could hang it in your temple space. Another expansive idea would be to share it and each take it home one night to sleep under, receiving everyone's blessings and ensuring sweet and prophetic dreams.

INTUITION ADVENTURE

This is one of my faves! Get together and write a list of "directions," something like:

1. Go to the crossroads.
2. Walk north for five minutes.
3. Take four steps to the left and look for a power object.
4. Walk south for 10 minutes.
5. Look to the sky for a sign.

The list is written purely spontaneously and intuitively - the idea is to see where you end up! It sounds bizarre, but try it and you'll see it's quite extraordinary.

CHAPTER 14

THE ART OF COVEN KEEPING

A coven is a sacred space - but it's also a shared space, and that means it comes with all the beauty and complexity of human interaction. While the magick is often what brings us together, it's the day-to-day decisions, shared responsibilities, and emotional intelligence that keep us together. Sometimes, despite everyone's best intentions, there will be disagreements and problems in your coven. This can lead to ego struggles and personality clashes. For situations like these, it is helpful to have some kind of governing body in place to mediate.

Having a governing body that can share leadership will facilitate a more harmonious and successful coven. Coven keeping is both an art and a commitment - and with care, honesty, and a bit of structure, it can be one of the most rewarding spiritual experiences of your life.

THE LEADER (OR LEADERS)

I always say that in the craft everyone ultimately leads themselves, but part of leading yourself is making smart decisions about being guided by those who have more knowledge and experience that you can benefit from. In a traditional coven, this would be the high priest and high priestess, but for an eclectic coven, I think a term that conveys a less hierarchical structure is more appropriate.

The roles of the leader or leaders can include:

★ Teaching the other coveners the ideology, skills, and practices of the craft, particularly pertaining to the coven's way of doing things.
★ Leading the rituals and spells of the meetings and suggesting "homework."
★ Keeping conversations between coveners moving harmoniously, making sure that everyone has a fair say and is heard and listened to.
★ Overseeing the spiritual health and growth of the coven as a whole.
★ Advising individuals on personal mental and emotional challenges that may be affecting their craft and encouraging positive development of themselves.

LEADERSHIP IN THE COVEN

When it comes to coven leadership, having two facilitators or leaders can be a powerful and balanced approach. These leaders might be female/male, same-sex, or non-binary, depending on the composition and preferences of the group.

Having two leaders in an eclectic coven has practical benefits as well. Sharing leadership allows for collaboration, mutual support, and the delegation of responsibilities, preventing burnout and ensuring the group functions harmoniously. This approach embodies the spirit of balance and connection that lies at the heart of the craft.

A TALKING STICK

A talking stick is a powerful tool for ensuring that everyone in the group has a fair say and feels truly heard, especially during emotional or heated discussions. The "stick" doesn't have to be a literal stick - it can be any clearly identifiable object, such as a crystal, a small cauldron, or even a decorative feather.

The principle is simple: as the talking stick is passed from person to person, only the person holding it may speak. This ensures that all voices are heard, especially in larger groups where individual contributions can sometimes be overshadowed. A great practice is to make sure everyone holds the talking stick at least once during a discussion, encouraging equal participation.

THE COORDINATOR

A coordinator is essential when the coven grows beyond three or four members and logistics become more complex. This person helps keep everything running smoothly, from scheduling meetings to organizing supplies, and they work closely with the leader to ensure plans are clear and well-executed.

The coordinator's role is to:

- ★ Assist the leader in planning rituals, events, and seasonal festivals.
- ★ Maintain a contact list for all coven members.
- ★ Use digital tools like email, messaging apps, or shared calendars to communicate dates, locations, and requirements.
- ★ Keep a record of successful venues for gatherings and manage the logistics of finding new ones.
- ★ Connect with local pagan and witchcraft communities to discover events the coven may want to attend or contribute to.
- ★ Collaborate with the money manager to ensure supplies for rituals and gatherings are well-stocked and appropriately funded.

THE MONEY MANAGER

This role involves handling the coven's finances and coordinating fundraising activities. As the group grows, it can be helpful to establish a small fund for shared expenses, such as ritual supplies, transportation, or venue rentals.

The money manager's role is to:

- ★ Collect and manage financial contributions from members.
- ★ Track spending and ensure transparency in financial matters.
- ★ Organize fundraising activities, such as selling crafts at festivals or hosting magickal workshops.
- ★ Maintain an inventory of the coven's pantry of magickal goods, including herbs, candles, and tools.
- ★ Suggest cost-effective ways to enhance gatherings or fund special projects, such as group retreats or workshops.

THE BOOK KEEPER

Updating the coven's Book of Shadows is an important and creative task. Having a dedicated person to manage this ensures the group's magickal history is preserved and accessible to all members.

The book keeper's role is to:

★ Record rituals, spells, member contributions, and other significant details in the coven's Book of Shadows.

★ Add artistic touches, such as illustrations, calligraphy, or pressed flowers, to make the book visually inspiring or coordinate contributions from coven members for artistic purposes.

★ Maintain a lending system for any shared coven resources, such as books or other materials.

★ Digitize important information for easy sharing among members, while keeping physical records for tradition.

THE ACTIVIST

The activist ensures the coven stays connected to the world through meaningful environmental and humanitarian efforts. This role fosters a sense of responsibility and action, aligning with the Wiccan principle of "harm none."

The activist's role is to:

- ★ Coordinate the coven's involvement in environmental causes, such as beach cleanups, tree planting, or wildlife conservation projects.
- ★ Maintain memberships in organizations like Greenpeace or local environmental groups.
- ★ Organize charity drives or volunteering efforts to support local or global causes.
- ★ Inspire the coven with ideas for magickal activism, such as rituals to heal the earth or raising awareness for social issues.

THE WEB KEEPER

In today's digital world, having an online presence can strengthen a coven's connection and cohesion. A web keeper (or web designer) can create and maintain a website or private online forum for members.

The web keeper's role is to:

- ★ Design and manage a coven website, including features like an online Book of Shadows or a private members' forum.
- ★ Ensure secure communication by using private platforms for sensitive discussions.
- ★ Share updates about events, rituals, and resources on social media or within the coven's digital space.
- ★ Use technology to keep the coven connected, especially when meeting in person is difficult due to things like inclement weather or physical distance between coven members.

IDENTIFYING HEALTHY DYNAMICS

When welcoming new members, trust your intuition. If someone's energy feels off or their behavior raises concerns, take it seriously. Look for individuals who contribute positively, respect others, and align with the group's shared values.

To screen potential members, consider using divination tools like pendulums or tarot cards to gain insight into their intentions. Keep in mind that the energy you project as a group - openness, fairness, and positivity - often shapes the behavior of those who join.

MAINTAINING YOUR SOLITARY PRACTICE

Even as a member of a coven, maintaining your solitary practice is vital. The benefits are immense, both for you as an individual and for the collective energy of the group. Personal insights, revelations, and suggestions brought by individual members keep the group dynamic, vital, and evolving.

Witches are individuals. We're not meant to think the same, share the same opinions, or express ourselves identically. In fact, our diversity is essential to the strength and richness of the group. So don't be alarmed if disagreements arise within a coven - it's a sign of healthy, independent thinking. However, if someone's behavior is less witch and more wanker, read on . . .

CONFRONTING CHALLENGES IN YOUR COVEN

Disagreements can arise in any group, including covens. When arguments start to dominate, it's crucial to pause and reconnect with your shared purpose. Reflect on why you formed the coven in the first place and what you hoped to achieve together. Consider meeting in a neutral, relaxing environment - like a beach or park - to revisit your initial enthusiasm and strengthen your bond.

Remember, obstacles can be opportunities for growth. Approach challenges with the intention of resolving them collectively. By working through difficulties, you'll emerge stronger as individuals and as a coven.

It's important to know that nudity or sexual rituals are never required in witchcraft, despite the myths. Your body and your personal choices are sacred, and no one has the right to exploit or pressure you. Always trust your instincts - if a situation feels uncomfortable, remove yourself immediately.

SETTING BOUNDARIES: ONLINE AND OFFLINE

When I was an administrator of the forum on my website, I had to take decisive action to maintain a positive and constructive space. I apply the same cut-the-crap approach on social media today. If someone is not supportive, respectful, or appropriate, I block and delete them. I will not hold space for negativity, and that is my right in my corner of the online universe.

WHEN SOMEONE CROSSES THE LINE

Whether online or in person, it's crucial to establish and maintain boundaries. In a coven, ensuring a safe, supportive environment is a collective responsibility. If someone's behavior becomes disruptive, it may be time to take action.

Thankfully, I was fortunate not to experience this firsthand - our coven was composed of mature, confident women who approached issues calmly and constructively. However, if conflicts do arise, they often stem from a lack of confidence. When someone feels the need to over-assert themselves or dominate discussions, it's usually a sign of insecurity - a cry for attention rooted in self-doubt.

It's essential to approach these situations with empathy and a clear mind. Sometimes, gentle guidance or encouragement can help someone find their place within the group. But if their behavior consistently disrupts the harmony and purpose of the coven, it might be time to have an honest discussion about whether they align with the group's energy and goals.

Here's a checklist to help identify when someone might need a warning - or even be asked to leave the group. If you answer yes to three items, consider issuing a severe warning. If four or more apply, it may be time to part ways:

- ★ Deliberately starts arguments that are not constructive.
- ★ Invades others' physical or emotional boundaries.
- ★ Makes unwanted sexual advances.
- ★ Insults or denigrates others personally or undermines their efforts.
- ★ Ignores concerns from coven members, especially the leader.
- ★ Repeatedly fails to participate in meetings or activities without good reason.

EXERCISING COMPASSION AND STRENGTH

While it's ideal to address issues with patience, compassion, and mutual respect, sometimes excommunication becomes necessary for the well-being of the group. Witches are healers, and sometimes healing begins by making someone aware of their behavior - even if it means asking them to leave.

When you decide someone must step away, stick to your decision. Set a clear time frame - six weeks is a good minimum - during which they are completely removed from the group. This creates space for reflection and demonstrates the seriousness of the boundaries.

If, after this period, they express a sincere desire to return and show growth, welcome them back with a joyful re-initiation ceremony. Celebrate their positive transformation and the strength gained by the coven through the process.

ENDING A COVEN

If the time comes to dissolve a coven, approach it with respect and intention. Hold a final gathering to honor the time you've spent together, sharing food, stories, and memories. Avoid casting a circle or performing magick during this meeting - focus instead on celebrating your shared journey.

For an amicable split, ensure that the coven's Book of Shadows and other shared items are kept safe. If the split is contentious, consider burying or safely burning items to release negativity and bring closure.

TRUSTING YOUR PATH

Your journey as a witch is deeply personal, and there's no "right" way to practice. Trust your instincts, follow what feels authentic to you, and remember that your faith doesn't need to be on public display. Whether you're sharing your path with others or keeping it private, your connection to the craft is valid and powerful.

FINAL THOUGHTS

The wisdom shared here reflects the unique journey of being a witch in a coven - a path of collective growth, shared magick, and mutual empowerment. Navigating group dynamics, celebrating diversity, and working together toward common goals are all part of what makes coven life transformative and rewarding.

A well-kept coven is not one without flaws, but one that learns, grows, and loves through them - holding space for magick, mess, and transformation in equal measure.

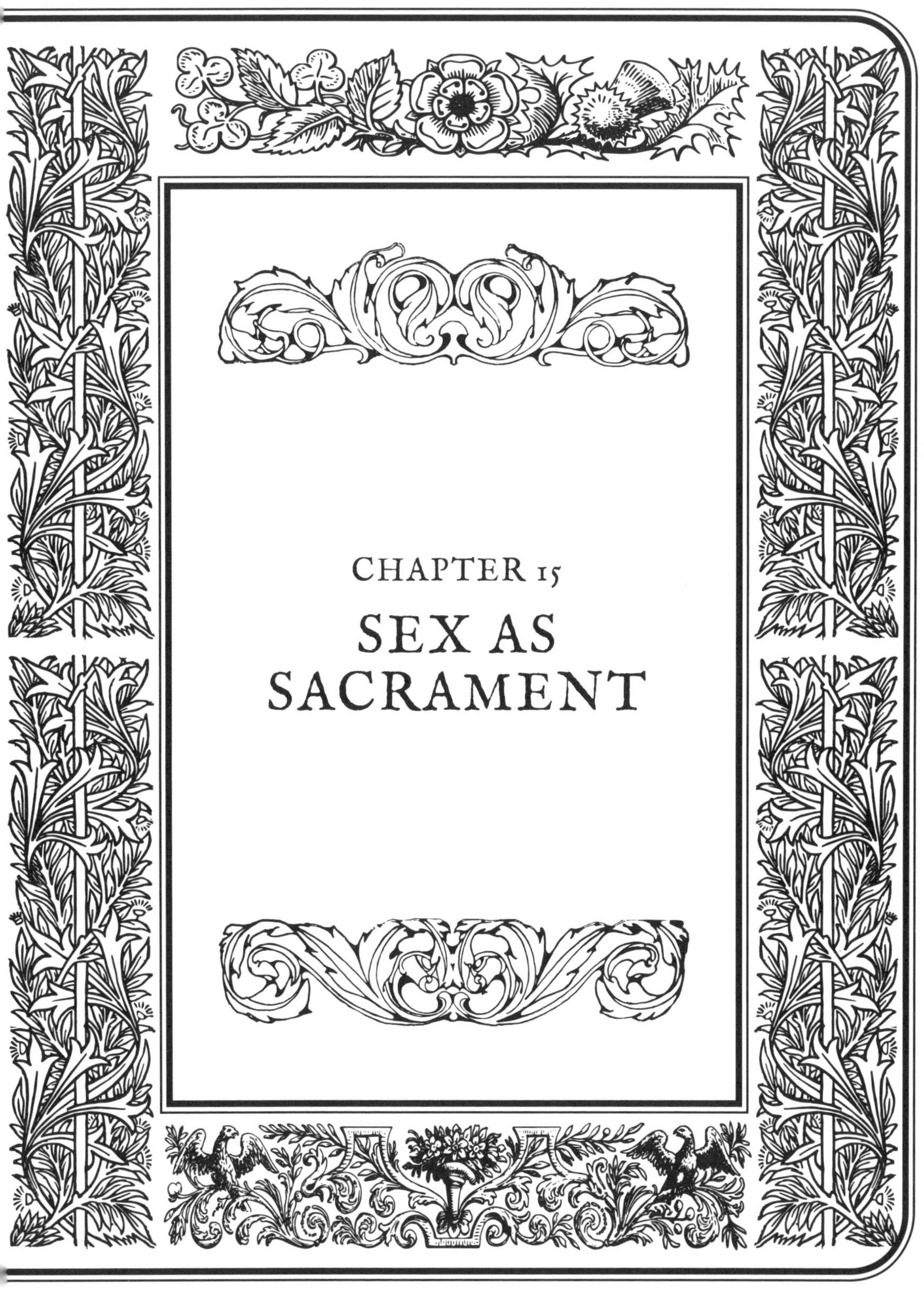

CHAPTER 15

SEX AS SACRAMENT

Witchcraft honors the sacredness of life, and sex is a vital, transformative aspect of that. It's an expression of creation, connection, and profound magick. If you've ever felt uneasy about your own sexuality or sensuality, it's worth exploring those feelings with compassion, because they can influence how you experience the craft.

Whether witches weave their sexual energy into rituals - alone, with a partner, or even within a group - or simply treat sexuality as a treasured and sacred part of life, this reverence for the physical self is central to our practice. Of course, this often leads to misrepresentation by those who either fear or exploit sexuality. They might claim witches and pagans have attitudes to sex that are wildly indulgent or inappropriate.

The truth is far more nuanced. Witches celebrate the blending of physical and spiritual joy, but how this manifests varies widely. You'll find monogamous, polygamous, celibate, gay, straight, bisexual, asexual, and every other expression of sexuality within the craft. Where witchcraft diverges from many spiritual paths is its refusal to claim that any one expression of sexuality is the only "right" way to live.

BALANCING LOVE AND FREEDOM

Witches actively work on minimizing negativity in our relationships to maximize joy and mutual respect. The Wiccan Rede reminds us: "An it harm none, do what ye will." This applies to our relationships, where we strive to balance our needs with those of our partners.

That said, conventional attitudes about sex and relationships can be deeply ingrained, making them hard to shake. For instance, how would you feel if your partner participated in a symbolic great rite with someone else as part of a Beltane ritual? Every witch's relationship with sex and ritual is deeply personal.

It's worth noting that rituals involving actual sex are far less common than sensationalists would have you believe. There is no obligation for anyone to participate in sexual rituals, and whether or not you choose to incorporate sexual energy into your magickal workings has no bearing on your power as a witch. Authentic sex magick only thrives when all participants are mature, grounded, and willing. Consent, respect, and intention are the foundation of this practice.

THE GREAT RITE

Historically, some witchcraft traditions included sexual rituals, often tied to fertility festivals. Ancient Beltane rites sometimes involved masked partners engaging in sacred unions to honor and ensure the fertility of the tribe and the land. These rituals were deeply spiritual, rooted in the understanding of communal survival.

In modern witchcraft, the great rite is most often symbolic. The union of masculine and feminine is represented by the chalice and the athame, signifying creation and balance. It's a magnificent expression of love, passion, and the interconnected forces that shape existence.

RAISING POWER WITH SEXUAL MAGICK

Witches understand the parallels between raising magickal power and sexual energy. The energy of a ritual can mirror the build-up, peak, and release of orgasm - an ecstatic cycle that channels transformative energy into the universe.

For solitary magickal workings, incorporating the energy of orgasm can amplify a spell's intent or seal a ritual. When shared between loving, committed partners, this energy is even more powerful, creating a deeply bonded and magickally charged connection.

The key is to treat sexual energy with reverence - aligning intention with the energy you're raising. If sex magick feels forced or purely indulgent, it's unlikely to serve its purpose.

PRACTICAL TIPS FOR SEXUAL MAGICK

- ★ START WHERE YOU'RE COMFORTABLE: If skyclad (naked) rituals feel daunting, begin by normalizing nudity in safe, private spaces. Over time, try experiences like skinny-dipping or attending a clothing-optional pagan event to ease into it.
- ★ COMMUNICATE OPENLY: If practicing with a partner, talk honestly about your comfort levels, desires, and boundaries. Mutual understanding and respect are essential.
- ★ DECONSTRUCT SHAME: Many people carry societal guilt about masturbation or sexual expression. Spend time exploring and enjoying your body, free of judgment, before incorporating these practices into ritual.
- ★ TAKE YOUR TIME: Whether solo or partnered, avoid rushing the experience. Raise energy slowly and intentionally, focusing on the power you're building rather than simply reaching orgasm.
- ★ PRACTICE TOGETHER: If you're working with a partner, spend time learning each other's preferences. Watch each other, pamper each other, and take time to cultivate trust and connection.

STUDYING AND CELEBRATING

The beauty of exploring sexual magick is that it places sex (so often exploited and commercialized) into the center of a sacred universe. Remember, though, that the aim isn't indulgence for its own sake, but rather empowerment, connection, and alignment with your highest intentions.

Sex is sacred, sensuality is magickal, and the human experience is enriched by embracing these truths. Whether you integrate sexual energy into your craft or simply hold it as a reverent aspect of life, remember: you are the ultimate authority over your body and your magick. Respect yourself, celebrate your passions, and let the power of your physical and spiritual self light your path.

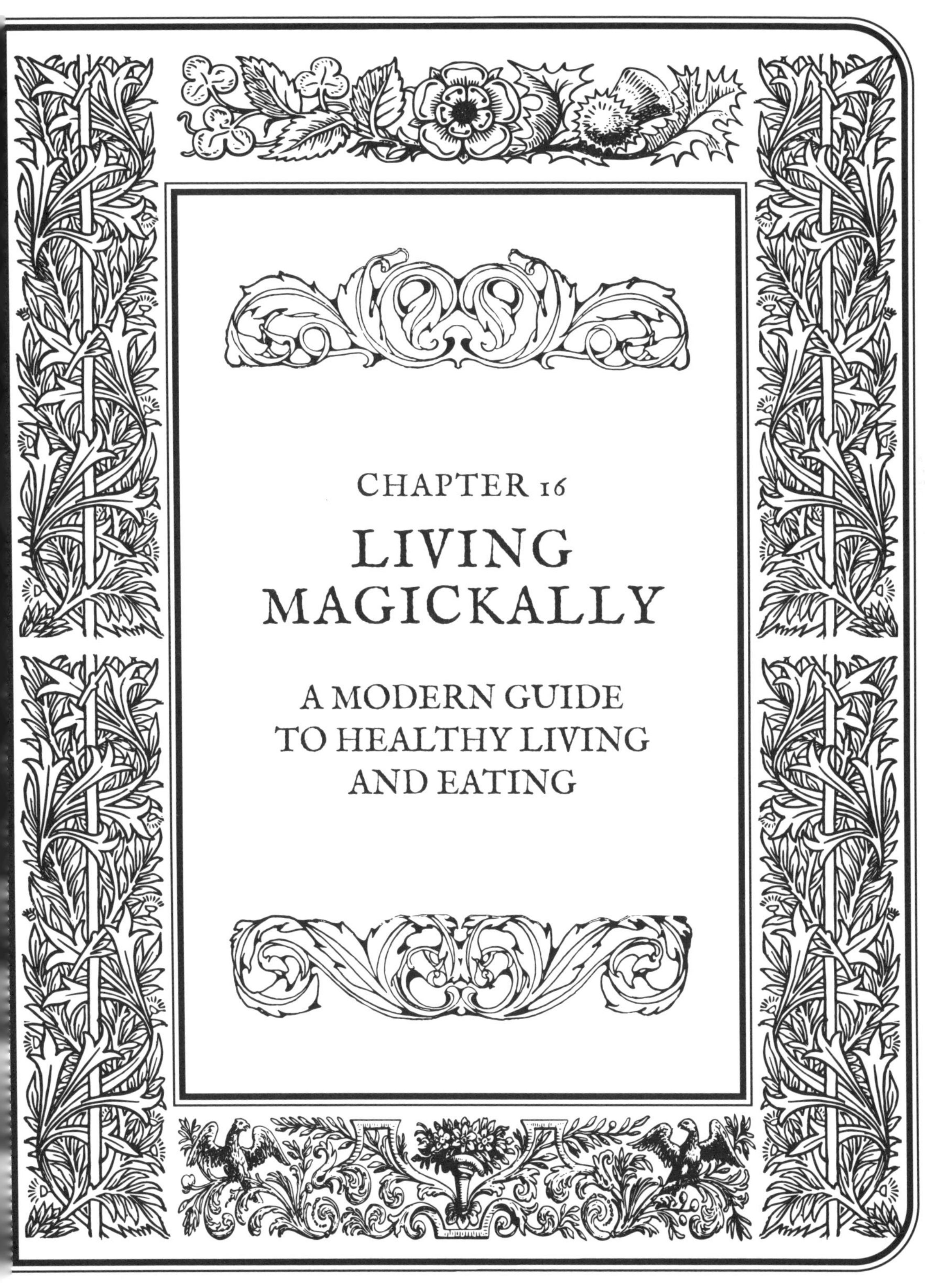

CHAPTER 16

LIVING MAGICKALLY

A MODERN GUIDE TO HEALTHY LIVING AND EATING

Being a witch is a 24/7 practice, and integrating mindful, sustainable lifestyle choices enhances your craft.

LIVING AND EATING WITH INTENTION

Healthy living begins with being mindful of how we treat ourselves, others, and the planet. This includes what we eat, how we move through the world, and the energy we bring to our craft. As a witch, you can embrace these principles:

- ★ Eat mindfully: Choose organic, locally sourced, and seasonal foods whenever possible. Avoid fast food and highly processed items, and instead view your meals as sacred acts of nourishment. For instance, savoring a salad of fresh greens or a steaming bowl of nourishing soup becomes a ritual of self-care.
- ★ Tread lightly: Reduce waste, recycle, and support ethical businesses. Buying from local farmers' markets or co-ops not only enhances your health but also strengthens your community.
- ★ Celebrate variety: Whether you're vegan, vegetarian, or an omnivore, honor your choices by eating with reverence. If you consume animal products, choose sustainably sourced, free-range, or wild-caught options. Respect the life that sustains you.

INCORPORATING HEALTHY EATING INTO YOUR CRAFT

Creating a coven "makeover" plan can be a fun and supportive way to collectively improve your eating habits. As a group, research local organic stores, vegan and vegetarian cafes, or co-ops and visit them together. Host potlucks with meals made from fresh, whole ingredients. Share recipes and cooking tips to inspire each other.

If you live alone or simply want to maintain a mindful kitchen, treat it as a temple. Stock it with wholesome foods, and prepare your meals with intention and love. Here are some essentials to guide your witchy eating habits.

Foods to embrace

Eat clean. Eat consciously. Let food be your ally.

- ★ **Seasonal plants:** Dark leafy greens, vibrant vegies, wild herbs, and fruits connect you to the earth's rhythm.
- ★ **Whole grains:** Quinoa, oats, millet, and brown rice fuel your body with steady energy.
- ★ **Healthy fats:** Choose cold-pressed olive or avocado oil, nuts, seeds, ghee, or coconut oil.
- ★ **Clean proteins:** Organic tofu/tempeh, beans, lentils, and seeds (hemp, chia, flax) nourish without excess processing.
- ★ **Intentional seasoning:** Use garlic, turmeric, ginger, and herbs for flavour and healing.
- ★ **Living water:** Drink filtered, spring, or mineral water. Infuse it with herbs, citrus, or intention.

Foods to minimize

Let what you eat elevate your energy, not dull it.

- ★ Ultra-processed foods: Skip long ingredient lists and artificial additives.
- ★ Refined sugar: Avoid hidden sugars. Choose raw honey, dates, or pure maple sparingly.
- ★ Industrial oils: Ditch refined seed oils (canola, soy, corn). Use cold-pressed oils instead.
- ★ White grains: Replace white flour and rice with whole, nutrient-rich alternatives.
- ★ Alcohol: If used, let it be ritual, not routine. Drink consciously.
- ★ Refined salt: Embrace mineral-rich salts. Avoid excessive iodized versions

BUILDING A COVEN PRACTICE AROUND HEALTHY LIVING

Host regular gatherings that encourage wellness and align with your magickal values. Here are some suggestions to get you started:

- ★ Cooking circles: Prepare meals together using fresh, seasonal ingredients. Add a magickal twist by incorporating herbs for prosperity or spices for protection.
- ★ Gardening: Start a coven garden, planting vegetables, herbs, and flowers that support your rituals and spells.
- ★ Community care: Volunteer for local environmental or food justice organizations as a coven.

Easy coven cooking

When it comes to post-circle feasts or Sabbat celebrations, simple, wholesome foods work best. One of my all-time favorites is a massive "everything but the kitchen sink" salad. Here's how I make it:

1. Start with a bag of pre-washed organic mixed salad leaves and toss them into a large bowl.
2. Add a handful of organic cherry tomatoes (red and yellow for extra color).
3. Chop up some organic pre-washed, pre-peeled baby carrots and throw those in too.
4. Dice a slab of teriyaki-baked organic tofu and add it, along with a handful of sprouted lentils, almond cheese, pine nuts, pepitas, or pecans.
5. Toss the salad with a couple of tablespoons of organic green goddess dressing and serve it with some pita bread and hummus.

This dish is quick, nutritious, and packed with love - perfect for a coven gathering.

I always recommend eating homemade dishes at these gatherings. Takeaway might be convenient, but it lacks the love and care that comes from food prepared by hand. Cooking is a form of alchemy, blending ingredients with intention to create nourishment for both the body and soul.

The supernaturally fit coven

Bonding outside of ritual is important for building a strong coven. Consider planning a fitness activity together, like a group hike to a beautiful natural location. Once you reach your destination, you can meditate as a group or raise power while enjoying the view.

My coven once planned a trek through Joshua Tree National Park. We worked up a sweat climbing the rugged trails and then meditated on the stark beauty of the desert. It was an unforgettable experience that connected us to the land and each other.

WITCHY HEALTH

Taking care of your physical and mental health is essential for maintaining a vibrant magickal practice. In my own life, I balance modern healthcare with natural remedies from around the world. One of my favorites is an organic herbal tea prescribed for me by a Bedouin doctor in Egypt, designed to calm the spirit and restore balance. I also use beautifully crafted essential oils made from indigenous Australian plants like lemon myrtle, eucalyptus, and tea tree. Lavender oil I sourced from the fields of Provence in France is my sleep charm. These oils bring the sacred energy of the land into my daily life and provide grounding and healing properties.

When I feel run down, I rely on natural supplements tailored to my needs, including evening primrose oil, coenzyme Q10, magnesium, turmeric, and vitamin C. A naturopath can guide you in choosing supplements to support your body and mind.

Stress can sneak into life in subtle ways, so consciously relax whenever possible. Pay attention to your posture, take deep breaths, and release tension when you feel it creeping in. Massage is another wonderful way to stay balanced and aligned. It stimulates lymph flow, enhances your chi, and helps with visualization - a vital skill for magickal workings.

Nourishing movement

Every morning, I dedicate 15 minutes to yoga. Poses like "salute to the sun" awaken my energy and help me connect with the earth and sky. I often pair these movements with music that inspires reflection - *Loveland* by Jai Uttal and Ben Leinbach has been a favorite for years.

Regular movement doesn't just strengthen your body - it aligns the physical with the spiritual. Whether it's yoga, tai chi, or a meditative walk, these practices create a strong foundation for your magick.

Personal good behavior

As a witch, cultivating a peaceful and empowered mind is fundamental to deepening your magickal practice. Beyond meditations and rituals, there are everyday ways to enhance your mental clarity and spiritual alignment, helping you become a stronger and more focused practitioner.

VISION MEDITATION

Take time to nourish your spirit with calming, inspiring visuals. Find a place with a stunning view - whether it's a mountaintop, beach, or city skyline - switch off your phone, and sit in quiet appreciation for 20 minutes or more. Alternatively, flip through a beautiful book filled with art or nature photography while playing soft, evocative music. These moments of quiet reflection can recharge your mind and ready you for powerful magickal work.

POSITIVE THOUGHTS, EMPOWERED MAGICK

Your thoughts influence your reality, so maintaining positivity is essential. If you find yourself spiraling into negativity, take a moment to pause. Light a white candle, burn some uplifting essential oils like lemon or clary sage, and focus on the good in your life. Reach out to your spiritual community or fellow witches for energetic support when needed - it's a powerful reminder that you're not alone on this journey.

TREAT YOURSELF LIKE A TEMPLE

Nurture your senses with small, sensual pleasures. Burn fragrant incense, light candles, or simply lie on a soft rug and appreciate how good it feels. Take time each day to enjoy life's simple, grounding moments.

CREATE A SANCTUARY AT HOME

Your home should be a haven of peace and magick. Avoid rushing to turn on the TV after work or school; instead, light candles, play soothing music, and spend a few moments at your personal altar or sacred space. Let your living space reflect the harmony and intention of your practice.

A few words on habits

- ★ Alcohol: If you indulge, reserve it for special occasions..
- ★ Drugs: They dull your senses and cloud your magick - leave them out of your practice.
- ★ Smoking: It's harmful to your body and the environment. Avoid it.

Final thoughts

Your body is your temple, and treating it with care enhances your magick. Listen to your body's needs, and balance movement, rest, and nourishment.

Healthy living isn't about perfection - it's about intention. Treat yourself with kindness and celebrate the small steps you take toward alignment with your magickal principles.

HEALING THE WORLD AS WITCHES

Is it too late to heal?

How do we live as witches in a world that often feels chaotic? Evidence shows that many aspects of society are improving, even if it doesn't always feel that way.

Reduce your exposure to fear-based media and seek out balanced reporting from trusted sources or spend your time on actions that promote peace and healing. Light candles, meditate, and direct your energy toward the change you wish to see. Conduct rituals for global healing and harmony. Remember, your thoughts and actions ripple outward, shaping the world in ways you might not immediately see.

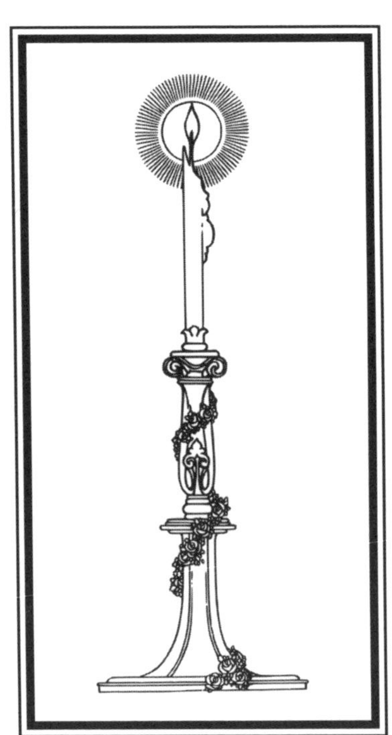

Environmental magick

Small actions can create significant changes. Start with mindful choices:

- ★ Reduce paper waste: Use both sides of paper for notes or drafts to cut your paper usage in half.
- ★ Support sustainable transportation: Choose hybrid or electric vehicles if possible, reducing emissions and contributing to a cleaner future. Or you could carpool, take public transport, or ride a bicycle.
- ★ Embrace eco-consciousness: Support businesses that prioritize sustainability, use eco-friendly cleaning products, and recycle thoughtfully.

Even when the challenges feel overwhelming, remind yourself that every small act matters. As witches, we honor nature as sacred and strive to tread lightly on the earth.

Community service and environmental activism

Your magick isn't just for the circle; it's for the world. Dedicate time to serving your community and protecting the environment:

- ★ Volunteer locally: Assist at youth shelters, food drives, or animal rescues. Sharing practical and magickal wisdom can be a powerful gift.
- ★ Support environmental causes: Participate in tree-planting events, sponsor endangered species, or join organizations like Greenpeace or Planet Ark.
- ★ Lead by example: Commit to using eco-friendly products, reducing waste, and inspiring others to do the same.

Let your daily practices reflect the respect and care you bring to your craft, and know that your dedication is a beacon of positive change in both your world and the greater one.

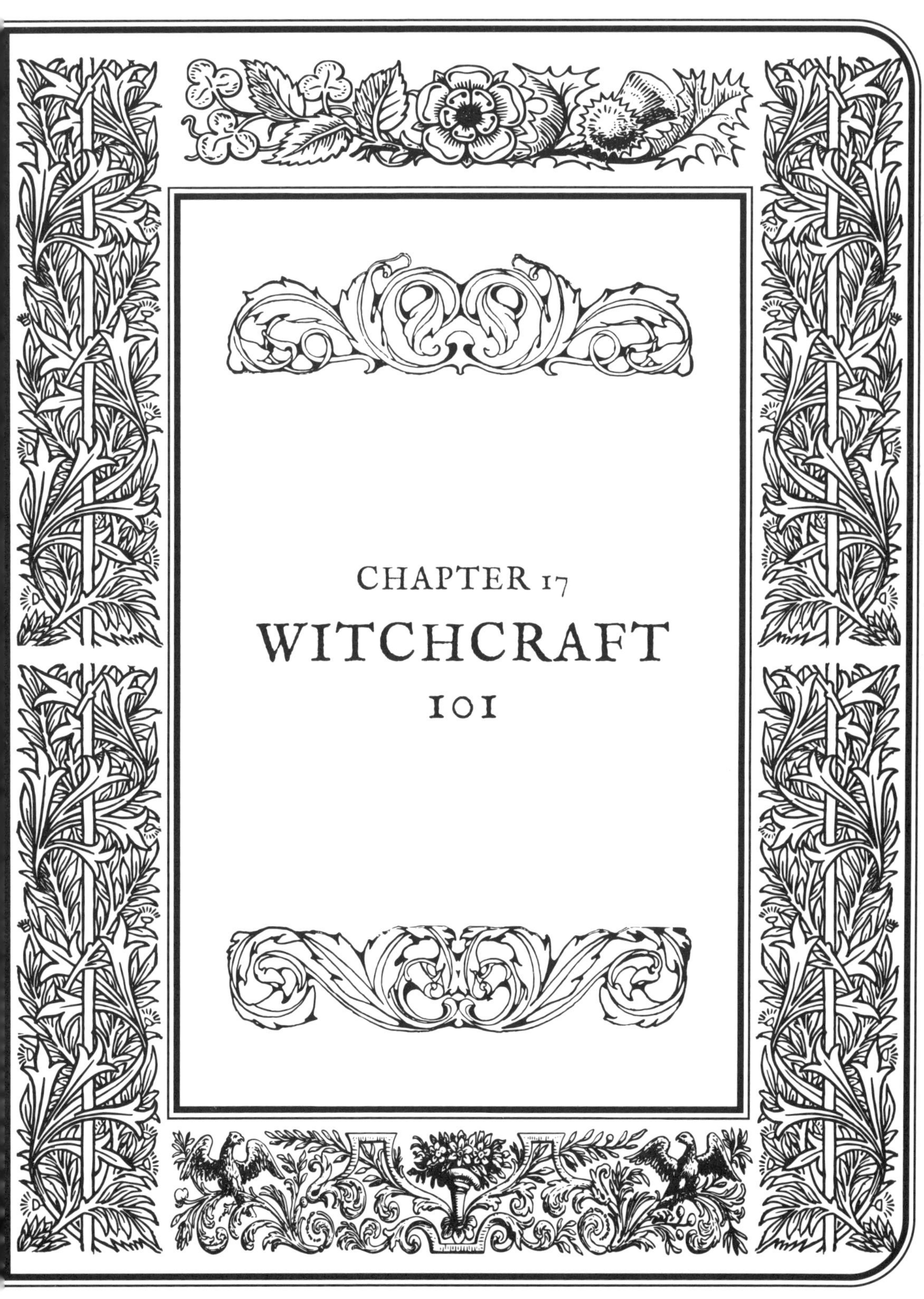

CHAPTER 17

WITCHCRAFT 101

In a traditional coven, an initiate is generally put through a course of formal education. This course may take the form of certain books they are told to read and then tested on. They may also be given a copy of the coven's Book of Shadows to study. Generally, this period of learning is called "first degree initiation" and it lasts for the period of a year and a day.

A year and a day may seem like a long time to be an initiate, but it's actually very short as far as time required for personal development and a "wisdom shift." What a witch knows isn't just about the information your rational brain has a handle on, but it also concerns inner knowledge, intuition, and psychic abilities that will evolve within you as you put that information into practice.

When you are starting your own eclectic coven it is a really good idea to have a similar course of formal study, so that you are all learning together. Some of you, of course, will know things that others don't and may feel like you're going over old ground - but a bit of revision never hurt anyone!

In witchcraft, the really important stuff is not so much the accumulation of facts and figures and formulas, but is more about a shift in consciousness, where the self awakens to a greater sense of evolutionary purpose and potential in every aspect of existence - physical, mental, emotional, spiritual, and magickal.

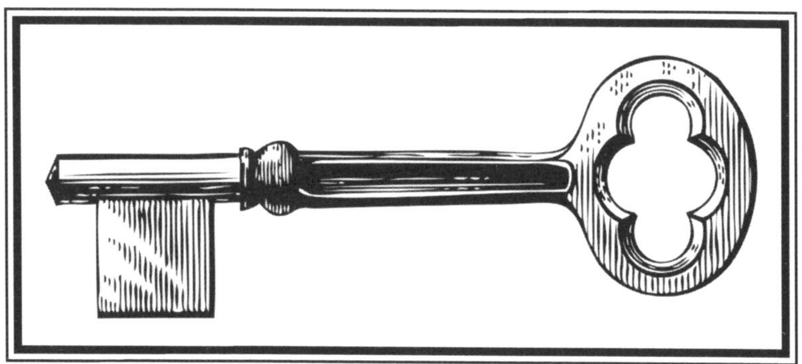

When putting together a formal course the lessons should be structured around the themes and concepts important to your practice and can include:

- ★ The lessons themselves, researching information, and writing up a personal report.
- ★ Practical and magickal exercises to develop the necessary magickal skills - for example, blending incense, making a money spell, or reading tarot cards.
- ★ A circle gathering/ritual to assist in absorbing the knowledge spiritually as well as intellectually.
- ★ An examination of sorts or a discussion to share knowledge to see if everyone, or just maybe a newcomer who is doing the course, is ready to progress to the next stage of initiation. So, if you are a witch who is hungry for knowledge, ready to work, and committed to achieving positive results, read on!

CRAFTING A COURSE IN WITCHCRAFT: COVEN MAGICKAL EDUCATION

When creating a course for learning witchcraft within a coven, it's important to blend tradition, modern practice, and creativity. A structured approach can deepen your collective knowledge, build trust among members, and prepare everyone for more complex magickal work. Below is an updated guide to designing a comprehensive coven course, emphasizing inclusivity, practicality, and modern witchcraft practices.

This eight-part course framework blends practical and spiritual lessons, fostering a holistic understanding of the craft. Each part incorporates research, hands-on practice, group discussions, and rituals.

Suggested course duration: Two to three weeks per part, with a fourth week dedicated to practical exams, discussions, and reflections.

Course outline

PART ONE: FOUNDATIONS OF WITCHCRAFT

- ★ UNDERSTANDING WITCHCRAFT: Dispel myths and misconceptions. Explore modern witchcraft as a spiritual path and its historical context.
- ★ LIVING WITCHCRAFT: Examine how witchcraft integrates into daily life. Study examples from diverse traditions to inspire your practices.
- ★ WITCH'S LAWS AND ETHICS: Discuss personal responsibility, the Wiccan Rede (even if you are not Wiccan), the Rule of Three, and the moral law (offered in my manifesto, *The Art of Witch*). Explore how these principles of the craft shape your actions and magickal intentions.
- ★ HISTORY OF WITCHCRAFT: Investigate ancient pagan traditions, the persecution of witches, and the evolution of modern witchcraft. Reflect on how the past influences the present.

PART TWO: TOOLS AND RITUALS

- ★ MAGICKAL TOOLS: Study the symbolism and use of the athame, wand, chalice, pentacle, cauldron, Book of Shadows, and more. Encourage members to create or consecrate their own tools.
- ★ SACRED SPACE AND CIRCLE-CASTING: Learn the art of creating sacred space, invoking the elements, and casting a circle. Explore the metaphysical and practical aspects of these rituals.

PART THREE: DIVINITY AND POWER

- Goddesses and gods: Examine divine archetypes and how they manifest in different cultures. Develop personal connections through meditation and visualization.
- Raising energy: Practice techniques for raising and directing energy, such as the cone of power, and explore how divine energy fuels magickal workings.

PART FOUR: THE WHEEL OF THE YEAR

- Sabbats and Esbats: Dive into the mythology, rituals, and seasonal significance of the Sabbats and lunar phases. Explore their relevance in modern life.
- Group celebrations: Plan rituals and activities for each holy day, emphasizing creativity and collaboration.

PART FIVE: SPELLCASTING AND MAGICKAL CRAFTING

- Spell creation: Learn the mechanics of spellcasting, including intent, timing, and energy alignment. Create personalized spells for love, prosperity, healing, and protection.
- Magickal crafting: Develop skills in blending herbs, oils, and powders; creating charms; and working with crystals and other sacred objects.

PART SIX: SHADOW WORK AND PROTECTION

- Dark magick: Understand the transformative power of shadow work. Explore topics such as protection magick, binding, banishing, and honoring cycles of death and rebirth.
- Psychic defense: Learn techniques for shielding against negativity and handling psychic attacks.

PART SEVEN: SPECIAL SKILLS

- ★ Divination: Study methods like tarot, astrology, pendulum work, and tea-leaf reading. Practice interpreting symbols and omens.
- ★ Dream work: Keep a dream journal and analyze recurring themes and symbols.
- ★ Astral projection: Learn techniques for out-of-body experiences and spiritual exploration.

PART EIGHT: LIFE AS A WITCH

- ★ Rites of passage: Study rituals for significant life events, such as handfastings, baby blessings, and crone/mother/maiden transitions.
- ★ Magickal living: Incorporate witchcraft into daily life through eco-conscious choices, healthy living, and mindfulness practices.
- ★ Pagan pride: Discuss ways to promote respect for modern witchcraft and contribute positively to the community. Take action to encourage respect and tolerance for witches and pagans. Go out into the world empowered and proud.

TIPS FOR A SUCCESSFUL COVEN STUDY PROGRAM

- ★ Collaborative learning: Assign members to research and present topics to the group to encourage shared responsibility and diverse perspectives.
- ★ Hands-on practice: Include plenty of practical exercises to apply lessons in real time, from casting circles to creating spell ingredients.
- ★ Customized resources: Compile readings, articles, and exercises into a shared coven manual or online resource for easy reference.
- ★ Group reflection: After each part of the course, hold a group discussion to share insights, experiences, and suggestions for improvement.

PERSONAL MAGICK AND COVEN HARMONY

Take your time with each step, and enjoy the journey. Witchcraft is not about finding the "right" answers but about embracing creativity, intuition, and growth - both individually and as a coven. Together, you will weave a web of magick and connection that is uniquely yours.

FINAL THOUGHTS

I have found over the years that I never stop learning, but as time progresses my comprehension becomes deeper and more profound and I cease to "remember things"; instead, I just "am" these things.

Take your time and enjoy this process, being as creative and imaginative as you desire. And remember, a lot of the time there won't be "right" and "wrong" answers as much as just people's different opinions and experiences, which should be respected and encouraged as they will create a fertile environment for your coven to grow and evolve.

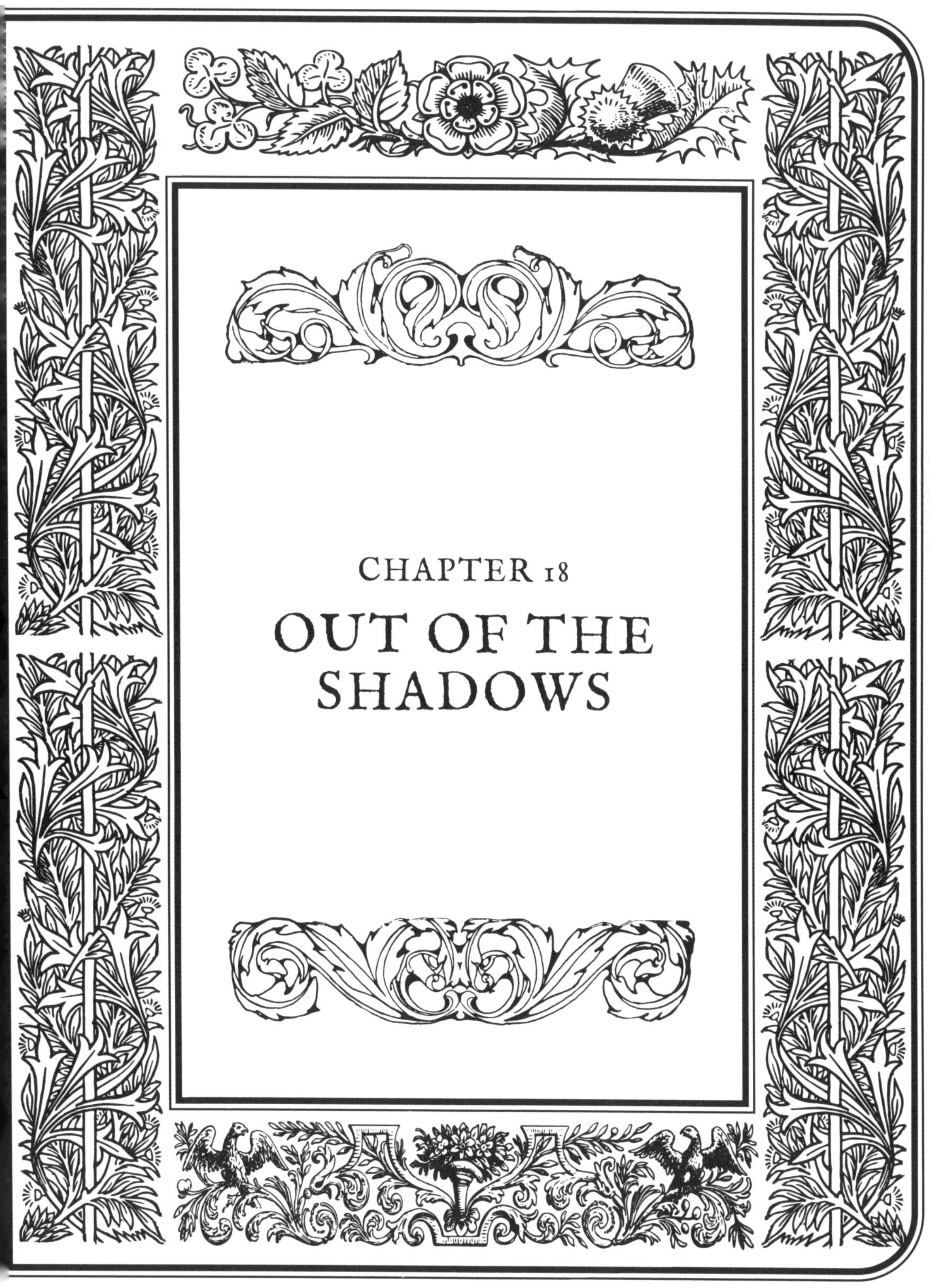

CHAPTER 18

OUT OF THE SHADOWS

As witches, part of our magickal journey often involves engaging with others, both within our community and beyond.

For some, discussing the craft publicly feels natural, while others prefer to keep their practices private. There's no right or wrong way - your comfort and boundaries come first. However, when you do choose to share, your authenticity and sincerity can inspire curiosity and respect, showing the world that witchcraft is about healing, empowerment, and connection.

EDUCATING AND ENGAGING WITH THE PUBLIC

Sharing the principles of witchcraft, in an informed and approachable way can help break stereotypes and shift perceptions from the "black magic" misconceptions to a more accurate understanding of the craft.

When engaging with others, focus on relatable themes - how rituals align with the cycles of nature or how mindfulness and meditation are integral to your practice. These ideas resonate universally, whether or not someone identifies as a witch.

SPELLCASTING AS CONNECTION

Performing spells for others is one way to extend the magickal practice beyond the circle, deepen connections and share the beauty of the craft.

A good example is creating a simple prosperity spell for someone who asks for help. Invite them to participate actively in the process - lighting a candle, chanting affirmations, or visualizing their goal. Their active involvement not only strengthens the spell but also introduces them to the intentionality and focus behind magick.

HOSTING INCLUSIVE AND MEMORABLE MAGICKAL MOMENTS

Sharing magick in a group setting can create unforgettable experiences. For example, hosting a small ritual or spellcasting during a gathering - such as lighting a candle for abundance or creating a vision board for collective goals - can transform a mundane event into something deeply meaningful.

These moments don't have to be elaborate: simply inviting loved ones to write intentions on paper and burn them as part of a release ritual can be profoundly impactful.

SETTING BOUNDARIES WITH MAGICKAL REQUESTS

When someone asks for a spell, it's important to assess their intentions and ensure that their request aligns with your ethical boundaries. Take time to understand their situation and explain how magick works. Empower them to be an active participant in the process, whether by lighting their own candle or crafting their own talisman with your guidance.

Remember, it's okay to say no if a request doesn't feel right. Protecting your energy and integrity is crucial. If you do choose to help, ensure there is an exchange of energy - whether through payment, a donation to charity, or a commitment to an act of kindness.

As you grow more adept in your craft, recognize that your work has value. Charging appropriately - whether in the form of money, bartering, or charitable exchange - creates balance and acknowledges the effort and expertise you bring to your magick.

FINAL THOUGHTS

Reaching out as a witch is about creating authentic connections, educating others with integrity, and honoring the value of your work. By setting clear boundaries, valuing your expertise, and sharing your magick with intention, you can inspire understanding and respect while staying true to yourself and your path.

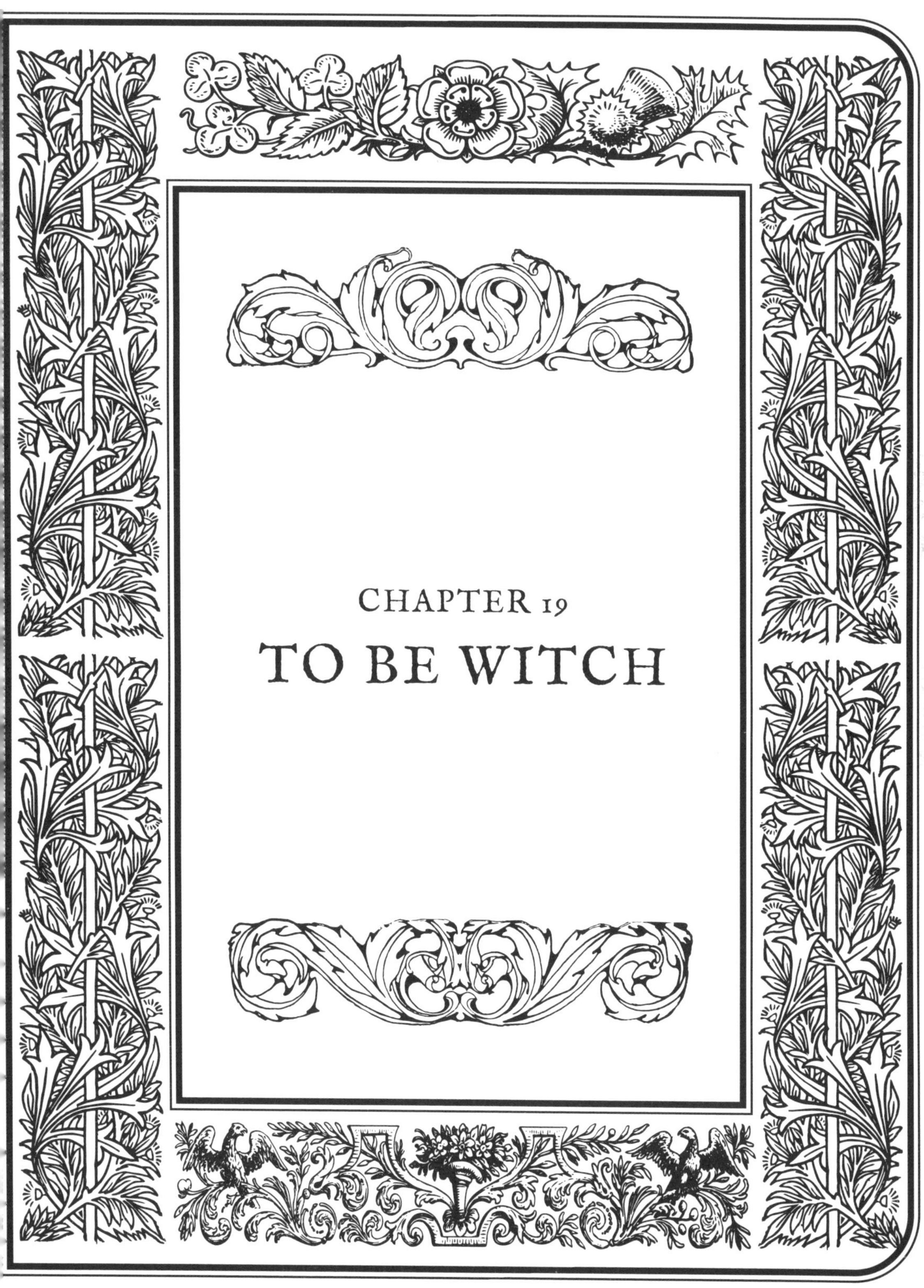

CHAPTER 19

TO BE WITCH

Public displays of witchcraft that are beautiful and fun definitely have a positive effect on the way people see us, so why not consider holding open circles and Sabbat celebrations in your area?

If you are setting up a public ritual from scratch yourself, make sure you get council approval beforehand. Contact your local council and explain that you would like to hold a spiritual meeting on public land; alternatively, sign up to participate in an already-established pagan festival.

If you are organizing a meeting or celebration yourself and want to let the community know about upcoming activities, post a notice in your local organic food co-op or at your local pagan/New Age book shop - anywhere you think like-minded people may congregate. Or post it on socials . . . lol.

Make sure that when you do the event you have some sort of security organized (like any public event) and make sure lots of your own friends are participating so that you have plenty of support!

THE EVOLUTION OF WILL IN WITCHCRAFT

I offered a public ritual where participants raised power by visualizing their desires and declaring "our will be done." While this practice was powerful and meaningful at the time, my perspective on will in witchcraft has evolved.

Now, I see will as more about being will-ing. It's about being willing to be of service. Willing to believe that something extraordinary is possible. Willing to feel deserving of blessings. Willing to open yourself to experience magick in its most profound and transformative forms.

Above all, it's about being willing to act with others' betterment, peace, and love in mind. A spell cast with pure intent, aligned with the well-being of all, will surely resonate with the universe, which conspires to make such harmony manifest.

True magick flows from this willingness - this openness to serve, to love, and to trust in the beauty of what can be.

ACTIVISM AND ADVOCACY FOR PAGAN RIGHTS

Engaging in political activism is essential to safeguard the rights of witches and pagans to practice their spirituality freely. In the United States, significant progress was made when the US military recognized Wicca in its Chaplain's Handbook, a milestone achieved through the efforts of organizations like the Covenant of the Goddess. Similarly, in Australia, laws prohibiting witchcraft were repealed progressively, starting with New South Wales in 1969, South Australia in 1991, Queensland in 2000, Victoria in 2005, and the Northern Territory in 2013. Despite these advancements, challenges in acceptance and respect persist.

Addressing ignorance with patience and compassion through gentle education is often effective. However, there are times when proactive measures, such as peaceful public demonstrations, contacting government officials, or organizing petitions to raise awareness about religious freedom, become necessary.

If you're a practicing witch or pagan, consider extending your activism to promote tolerance and acceptance for your community. a good starting point is to connect with established pagan organizations. Here are some notable groups in Australia and the United States:

Pagan Awareness Network Inc. (PAN)

Based in Sydney, Australia, PAN has been dedicated to educating the public about paganism and advocating for the rights of pagans since 1997.

Pagan Federation International (PFI) Australia

Part of a global organization founded in 1971, PFI Australia works to provide information, counter misconceptions about paganism, and support the rights of pagans to worship freely.

Covenant of the Goddess (CoG)

One of the largest and oldest Wiccan religious organizations, CoG has been instrumental in advocating for Wiccan rights, including the inclusion of Wicca in the US military's Chaplain's Handbook.

Aquarian Tabernacle Church (ATC)

Founded in 1979 and based in the United States, the ATC is a Wiccan church that has received full legal recognition in both the US and Australia. It offers various programs, including a Wiccan seminary.

Pagan Federation International (PFI) USA

PFI USA serves as an international complement to local and national pagan networking groups, aiming to connect pagans across the US and globally.

By reaching out to these organizations, you can learn about current initiatives and find opportunities to contribute to the ongoing efforts toward religious freedom and acceptance for all pagans and witches.

#PREACH . . . !

Witches don't proselytize, and none of the above suggestions should involve preaching. But, if there is one witchy responsibility that could be seen as a little like preaching and extends out of our immediate circle it is this - to keep people aware of all the good things in life, sharing the idea that heaven is here on earth.

Educate those who would throw up their hands and say, "What's the point of caring about the environment and each other and finding magick in the world? It's going to ruin!"

Let them know that violence is on the decrease in our communities, that environmental issues are being addressed, and that positive progress is being made.

Put some positive reinforcement out there and people will feel more compelled to take action in their everyday lives because they are being encouraged to see that an individual can make a difference. Our smallest thoughts and actions really do add up to create the world in which we live.

As a witch, preach love, preach strength, and share the magick of our craft!

CHAPTER 20

FINAL REFLECTIONS: THE JOURNEY CONTINUES

As this book draws to a close, I want to express my deepest gratitude to you, dear reader, for walking this path with me. Witchcraft, and especially the power of working in a coven, is about connection - not just to each other, but to ourselves, to the earth, and to the magick that weaves through all existence. This book is not the end of that connection, but rather a beginning.

To deepen and expand your journey, I feel blessed to share that I have created *The Coven Oracle* - a collection of oracle cards designed to complement the practices and themes explored in this book. These cards will provide insight, guidance, and a touch of magick to your daily life, whether you are working in a group or solo.

For those seeking transformative, nourishing experiences beyond the pages, I invite you to join me on a Meet Yourself adventure. These bespoke journeys are curated to awaken your spirit and immerse you in the sacred, whether it's exploring ancient temples in Egypt, the lush landscapes of Bali, or other soul-stirring destinations. Traveling with intention and connection is one of the most profound ways to align with the magick of life. Find out more at fionahorne.com.

And if this book has ignited a spark for more knowledge or exploration, you'll find that flame fanned in my other works. From practical guides to the craft, to spells, rituals, and personal reflections, each book is infused with the intention to inspire, empower, and uplift.

Your journey is uniquely yours, and it doesn't need to look like anyone else's. Wherever your path leads, may it be one of discovery, joy, and empowerment. Thank you for allowing me to be a light on it.

With love and magick,

Fiona

ABOUT THE AUTHOR

Fiona Horne is one of the world's most respected and influential modern witches. Over the past three decades, she has authored sixteen bestselling books and created four oracle decks that have shaped the evolution of the craft. Her commitment to dispelling harmful myths has helped witches today practice freely and without fear.

In the 1990s, Fiona rose to fame as the lead singer of Australian electro-rock band Def FX and built a prominent career in television and radio. After relocating to the USA, she continued her media work internationally. She is also a licensed commercial pilot, animal rescuer, and creator of spiritual retreats in Egypt and Bali, known as the Meet Yourself adventures.

Her 2025 release *The Lost Book of Spells* sold out its first print run in a month. *The Art of Witch* (2019) introduced a generation to witchcraft rooted in service and self-awareness, while *Teen Magick* (2021) remains a classic for young witches. Fiona's books are trusted companions - guiding readers to live magickally with purpose, integrity, and heart.

fionahorne.com | captainfifi | fionahorneofficial

ALSO BY FIONA HORNE

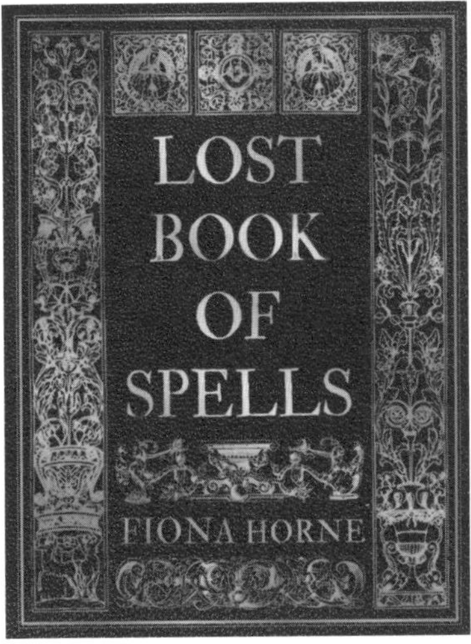

Lost Book of Spells
ISBN: 9781923009592

Coven Oracle
ISBN: 9781922468017